T0254994

Lecture Notes in Computer Science   13594

More information about this series at https://link.springer.com/bookseries/558

Xiang Li · Jinglei Lv · Yuankai Huo · Bin Dong ·
Richard M. Leahy · Quanzheng Li (Eds.)

Multiscale Multimodal Medical Imaging

Third International Workshop, MMMI 2022
Held in Conjunction with MICCAI 2022
Singapore, September 22, 2022
Proceedings

 Springer

Editors
Xiang Li ⓘ
Massachusetts General Hospital
Boston, MA, USA

Yuankai Huo ⓘ
Vanderbilt University
Nashville, TN, USA

Richard M. Leahy ⓘ
University of Southern California
Los Angeles, CA, USA

Jinglei Lv ⓘ
University of Sydney
Sydney, Australia

Bin Dong
Peking University
Beijing, China

Quanzheng Li ⓘ
Massachusetts General Hospital
Boston, MA, USA

ISSN 0302-9743   ISSN 1611-3349 (electronic)
Lecture Notes in Computer Science
ISBN 978-3-031-18813-8   ISBN 978-3-031-18814-5 (eBook)
https://doi.org/10.1007/978-3-031-18814-5

This Springer imprint is published by the registered company Springer Nature Switzerland AG
The registered company address is: Gewerbestrasse 11, 6330 Cham, Switzerland

Preface

On behalf of the organizing committee, we welcome you to the 3rd International Workshop on Multiscale Multimodal Medical Imaging (MMMI 2022), held in conjunction with the International Conference on Medical Image Computing and Computer Assisted Intervention (MICCAI 2022) in Singapore. The workshop was organized through the combined efforts of the Massachusetts General Hospital and Harvard Medical School, the University of Southern California, Peking University, Vanderbilt University, and the University of Sydney.

This series of MMMI workshops aims to develop the state of the art in acquiring and analyzing medical images at multiple scales and from multiple modalities. Topics of the workshop include algorithm development, implementation of methodologies, and experimental studies. The workshop also aims to facilitate more communication and interchange of ideas between researchers in the fields of clinical study, medical image analysis, and machine learning.

Since the first edition in 2019 (Shenzhen, China), the MMMI workshop has been well received by the MICCAI community. This year, the workshop's theme was novel methodology development for multi-modal fusion. MMMI 2022 received a total of 18 submissions. All submissions underwent a double-blind peer-review process, each being reviewed by at least two independent reviewers and one Program Committee (PC) member. Finally, 12 submissions were accepted for presentation at the workshop, which are included in this proceedings, based on the PC review scores and comments. The time and efforts of all the PC members and reviewers, which ensured that the MMMI workshop would feature high-quality and valuable works in the field, are highly appreciated.

With the increasing application of multi-modal, multi-scale imaging in medical research studies and clinical practice, we envision that the MMMI workshop will continue to serve as an international platform for presenting novel works, discussing essential challenges, and promoting collaborations within the community. We would like to thank everyone for the hard work, and see you next year!

September 2022

Xiang Li
Jinglei Lv
Yuankai Huo
Bin Dong
Richard M. Leahy
Quanzheng Li

Organization

Workshop Chairs

Xiang Li	Massachusetts General Hospital, USA
Jinglei Lv	University of Sydney, Australia
Yuankai Huo	Vanderbilt University, USA
Bin Dong	Peking University, China
Richard M. Leahy	University of Southern California, USA
Quanzheng Li	Massachusetts General Hospital, USA

Program Committee

Dakai Jin	PAII Inc., USA
Donghao Zhang	Monash University, Australia
Eung Joo Lee	Massachusetts General Hospital and Harvard Medical School, USA
Georgios Angelis	University of Sydney, Australia
Hui Ren	Massachusetts General Hospital and Harvard Medical School, USA
Jiang Hu	Massachusetts General Hospital and Harvard Medical School, USA
Lei Bi	University of Sydney, Australia
Liyue Shen	Stanford University, USA
Mariano Cabezas	University of Sydney, Australia
Shijie Zhao	Northwestern Polytechnical University, China
Zhoubing Xu	Siemens Healthineers, USA

Contents

M²F: A Multi-modal and Multi-task Fusion Network for Glioma Diagnosis and Prognosis

Zilin Lu[1,2], Mengkang Lu[2], and Yong Xia[1,2(✉)]

[1] Ningbo Institute of Northwestern Polytechnical University, Ningbo 315048, China
[2] National Engineering Laboratory for Integrated Aero-Space-Ground-Ocean Big Data Application Technology, School of Computer Science and Engineering, Northwestern Polytechnical University, Xi'an 710072, China
yxia@nwpu.edu.cn

Abstract. Clinical decision of oncology comes from multi-modal information, such as morphological information from histopathology and molecular profiles from genomics. Most of the existing multi-modal learning models achieve better performance than single-modal models. However, these multi-modal models only focus on the interactive information between modalities, which ignore the internal relationship between multiple tasks. Both survival analysis task and tumor grading task can provide reliable information for pathologists in the diagnosis and prognosis of cancer. In this work, we present a Multi-modal and Multi-task Fusion (M²F) model to make use of the potential connection between modalities and tasks. The co-attention module in multi-modal transformer extractor can excavate the intrinsic information between modalities more effectively than the original fusion methods. Joint training of tumor grading branch and survival analysis branch, instead of separating them, can make full use of the complementary information between tasks to improve the performance of the model. We validate our M²F model on glioma datasets from the Cancer Genome Atlas (TCGA). Experiment results show our M²F model is superior to existing multi-modal models, which proves the effectiveness of our model.

Keywords: Multi-modal learning · Multi-task · Survival analysis · Tumor grading

1 Introduction

Gliomas are the most common primary malignant brain tumors, which account for 80% of cases [26]. Clinical diagnosis and prognosis of gliomas comes from multi-modal information, such as pathological images and genomics data [7]. Pathological images contain the structural and morphological information of tumor cells, and genomics data provide molecular profiles.

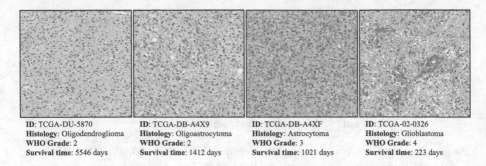

ID: TCGA-DU-5870	**ID**: TCGA-DB-A4X9	**ID**: TCGA-DB-A4XF	**ID**: TCGA-02-0326
Histology: Oligodendroglioma	**Histology**: Oligoastrocytoma	**Histology**: Astrocytoma	**Histology**: Glioblastoma
WHO Grade: 2	**WHO Grade**: 2	**WHO Grade**: 3	**WHO Grade**: 4
Survival time: 5546 days	**Survival time**: 1412 days	**Survival time**: 1021 days	**Survival time**: 223 days

Fig. 1. Some representative ROIs with gliomas. Necrosis and the abnormal microvascular structures are common in patients with high-grade gliomas, which are often used for grading. For patients, high-grade gliomas represent shorter survival.

With the rapid development of artificial intelligence technology, more and more models based on deep learning have been proposed for multi-modal learning in gliomas diagnosis and prognosis. However, pathological images and genomics data have great heterogeneity, which are different in dimension and expression. An effective fusion strategy is the key to effectively utilize heterogeneous multi-modal data [1,18]. There are different fusion strategies for cancer diagnosis or prognosis. Morbadersany et al. [17] utilized vector concatenation to combine pathological images and genomics information for cancer diagnosis. Chen et al. [4] proposed a multi-modal framework which adopted Kronecker Product to fuse pathology and genomics for survival analysis or grade classification. Similarly, Braman et al. [2] extended the Kronecker product with additionally radiology and clinical data for tumor prognosis.

Besides these operation-based methods, attention-based methods [23] has shown potential in the filed of multi-modal learning, which have been widely used in multi-modal learning task. In the field of visual question answering, Kim et al. [12] proposed bilinear attention networks to learn the richer joint representation for multi-modal input. Kim et al. [13] proposed the ViLT, a minimal vision and language pre-training architecture, to focus on the modality interactions inside the transformer module. In pathology field, Chen et al. [5] proposed a genomic-guided co-attention module that could learn how genes affect survival diagnosis. Wang et al. [25] designed an asymmetrical multi-modal attention mechanism to obtain a more flexible multi-modal information fusion for prognosis. However, the models mentioned above only focus on one task and ignore the correlation of different tasks.

Traditionally, deep learning networks tackle tasks in isolation, which are redundant in parameters and ignore the correlation of tasks. Compared with single-task learning, Multi-task learning (MTL) has the potential to improve performance by sharing the complementary information between tasks [22]. Sun et al. [20] integrated semantic segmentation and surface normal prediction tasks into a multi-task learning framework. Vafaeikia et al. [21] added a genetic alteration classifier as an auxiliary task to improve the accuracy of the segmentation results. The diagnosis and prognosis of gliomas can also be integrated into a multi-task learning paradigm. Both survival analysis task and tumor grading task can provide reliable information for pathologists. Predicting survival outcome is a standard method for cancer prognosis, which can be used to predict treatment response and help pathologists make early decisions [24]. In the summary of 2021 World Health Organization (WHO) classification of tumors of the Central Nervous System [15], gliomas can be divided by malignancy into grade 2–4. Tumor grading task is to predict the tumor grade through the malignancy, which has crucial significance for pathologists to make treatment plan and risk stratification. Furthermore, there is a correlation between the survival analysis task and the tumor grading task. Generally, the malignant degree of tumor is inversely proportional to the survival time of patients as shown in the Fig. 1.

In this paper, we propose a multi-modal and multi-task deep learning model, called **Multi-modal Multi-task Fusion** (M²F), to combine pathological and genomics data for the diagnosis and prognosis of gliomas. The main contributions of this paper are three-fold:

- We integrate the multi-modal learning and multi-task learning into one framework to simultaneously use the power of multiple modalities and tasks. The experiments on glioma datasets show effectiveness of our framework.
- We propose a multi-modal co-attention module, which could learn the complementary information to guide different modality learning.
- We train our M²F model for survival analysis task and tumor grading task jointly, which improves the accuracy of prediction by fully mining the potential correlation information between tasks.

2 Methods

The overall framework of our M²F model is shown in Fig. 2. M²F is a three-stage deep learning framework that effectively utilizes the correlation and complementarity information between multi-modal data and multiple tasks, including (1) Unimodal Feature Extraction, (2) Multi-modal Transformer Encoder, and (3) Tasks Mutual-Guided Mechanism. Suppose that $X = [x_1, x_2, \ldots, x_M]$ (M is the number of modalities) represents the data for a patient diagnosis and prognosis. In stage 1, a unimodal network accepts x_m and generates feature embedding h_m for each modality m. Then our Multi-modal Transformer Encoder learns joint representations h_{fusion} via measuring the correlation between modalities in stage 2 and h_{fusion} is finally used for diagnosis and prognosis in stage 3.

2.1 Unimodal Feature Extraction

Due to unique characteristics of each modality, we design different unimodal feature extraction networks for each modality.

Pathological Images. Pathological images have been an important tool in cancer diagnosis and prognosis for a century and pathologists widely use them in clinical decision [8]. Yet, gigapixel whole slide image (WSI) cannot be processed

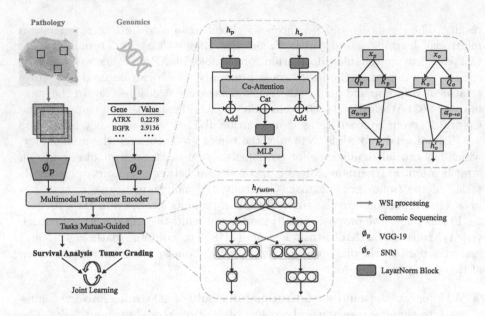

Fig. 2. The framework of M^2F. The left part is the overall process and the right there boxes are specific structure of our modules. M^2F train unimodal feature extraction networks firstly and then train multi-modal network using unimodal feature extractors. Multi-modal fusion task is performed by co-attention module to fuse feature embeddings from multiple modalities. Finally, fusion features are used for the jointly training of multiple supervised learning tasks.

directly because of the huge amount of calculation. To reduce the calculation and focus on informative regions, we used 1024×1024 region-of-interests (ROIs) at $20\times$ objective magnification from WSIs cropped by [17]. To extract features from pathological images, we used a VGG-19 [19] as feature extractor which is pre-trained on the ImageNet and fine-tuned on ROIs. The output of VGG-19 last hidden layer is pathological features $h_p \in \mathbb{R}^{d \times 1}$ which are part of the input of Multi-modal Transformer Encoder.

Genomics Data. Genomics data such as copy number variation (CNV), gene mutation status, and RNA sequencing (RNA-Seq) is also an important analytical tool in cancer diagnosis and prognosis [10]. However, genomics data has high dimensionality but small sample size for network training, which makes it easy to overfit during training. We use Self-Normalizing Network (SNN) [14] to extract genomics features $h_o \in \mathbb{R}^{d \times 1}$, which is also part of input of Multi-modal Transformer Encoder. SNN can induce variance stabilization to avoid gradients exploding and vanishing, which can mitigate overfitting.

2.2 Multi-modal Transformer Encoder

In order to capture the joint representation between pathological features and genomics features, we propose a Multi-modal Transformer Encoder (MTE) that fuses embeddings of each modality into joint representation $h_{fusion} = \Phi(h_p, h_o) \in \mathbb{R}^{2d \times 1}$, where Φ represents the MTE. The co-attention module utilize the correlation and complementarity between modalities to generate fusion futures.

Co-attention. Inspired by [16], Co-attention mechanism connect the pathological and genomics data by calculating the similarity between features. h_p and h_o are the input of mechanism and represent the embedding of pathological and genomics data, respectively. The output of co-attention is computed as follows:

$$h'_p = \alpha_{o \to p}(W_V h_p) \in \mathbb{R}^{d \times 1} \tag{1}$$

$$h'_o = \alpha_{p \to o}(W_V h_o) \in \mathbb{R}^{d \times 1} \tag{2}$$

where $\alpha_{o \to p}$ and $\alpha_{p \to o}$ are the weight coefficients calculated by multiplying two vectors:

$$\alpha_{o \to p} = \text{softmax}(\frac{W_Q h_o (W_K h_p)^T}{\sqrt{d}}) \in \mathbb{R}^{d \times d} \tag{3}$$

$$\alpha_{p \to o} = \text{softmax}(\frac{W_Q h_p (W_K h_o)^T}{\sqrt{d}}) \in \mathbb{R}^{d \times d} \tag{4}$$

where $W_Q, W_K, W_V \in \mathbb{R}^{d \times d}$ are trainable weight matrices. Thus we obtain the hidden representations h'_p and h'_o under mutual guidance between modalities.

We concatenate h'_p and h'_o into a matrix $h'_{fusion} \in \mathbb{R}^{2d \times 1}$. Then a two-layer multi-layer perceptron (MLP) is employed to learn a joint representation. Meanwhile, Layernorm (LN) is applied before every block and residual connection [9] is also applied throughout the process as follows:

$$h_{fusion} = \text{MLP}(\text{LN}(h'_{fusion})) + h'_{fusion} \tag{5}$$

where $h_{fusion} \in \mathbb{R}^{2d \times 1}$ is the input of downstream network.

2.3   Tasks Mutual-Guided Mechanism

In this section, we use MTL with hard parameter sharing strategy to learn the correlation between tumor grading task and survival analysis task. As shown in the Fig. 2, we design two separated heads for each task after a sharing MLP block. Except the sharing MLP block, we also add interaction between two separeted heads. When the main task is determined, we concatenate the auxiliary task to the main task header to improve the results of main task, which called Tasks Mutual-Guided Mechanism (TMG). TMG can be written as:

$$\begin{cases} h_s^2 = \text{Cat}(\text{MLP}(h_s^1), \text{MLP}(h_g^1)) & \text{main task: survival analysis} \\ h_g^2 = \text{Cat}(\text{MLP}(h_g^1), \text{MLP}(h_s^1)) & \text{main task: tumor grading} \end{cases} \tag{6}$$

and then h_s^2 and h_g^2 are used to predict the results of diagnosis and prognosis.

The loss function is used in multi-task networks consists of two parts, the negative log partial likelihood loss for survival analysis and cross entropy loss for tumor grading. Similar to [11], we compute the loss function as follows:

$$\mathcal{L}_{\text{cox}} = \sum_{i:R(t_i)=1} \left(-o_i + \log \sum_{j:t_j \geq t_i} \exp\left(o_j\right) \right) \tag{7}$$

where o_i is the risk prediction value of the network for the i patient, $R(t_i)$ value is 1 means that the i patient has occurred the event of interest (*i.e.*, died), the value is 0 if the patient is still alive at the last visit, and j represents the set of survival times less than i. The overall loss is:

$$\mathcal{L} = \lambda_{\text{cox}} \times \mathcal{L}_{\text{cox}} + \lambda_{\text{ce}} \times \mathcal{L}_{\text{ce}} \tag{8}$$

where λ_{cox} and λ_{ce} represent the weights of the negative log partial likelihood loss function and the cross entropy loss function, respectively. As the main task and auxiliary task are exchanged, the weights of the two losses will also be adjusted accordingly.

2.4   Implementation and Evaluation

Following [4], the unimodal networks are trained firstly for 50 epochs with low learning rate and a batch size of 8. After training this unimodal networks, we train our multi-modal network for 30 epochs with a batch size of 32. The embedding size d of unimodal networks is set to 32.

The concordance index (C-index) is used to evaluate the performance in survival analysis, and the accuracy (Acc), area under the curve (AUC), and F1-score are used to evaluate the performance in tumor grading.

3   Datasets

To validate the proposed M^2F model, we used two projects from the Cancer Genome Atlas (TCGA), *i.e.*, TCGA-GBM and TCGA-LGG. TCGA is a public cancer data consortium that contains paired diagnostic WSIs and genomics data with ground-truth survival times and histoloigic grade lables. We adopted the 1459 normalized ROIs cropped by [17]. Each subject has at least one WSI and each WSI had 1–3 ROIs. Hence, there are totally 1019 WSIs for 736 subjects. The genomics data of each subject consists of 320 features, including one mutation status, 79 CNV, and 240 RNA-Seq from TCGA and eBioPortal [3]. We conducted a 15-fold Monte-carlo cross-validation using the patient-level data split provided in [17].

4 Results and Discussion

To validate our fusion module effectiveness, we compare our fusion approach to prior approaches for the fusion of pathology and genomics (Table 1) with using multi-task learning strategy. And the ablation experiments of multi-task learning strategy are in Table 2. To ensure the fairness of the experimental setup, we use the identical train-test split with previous models [4,17]. Pathomic Fusion is open-sourced and all of this results are reproduced based on open codes and data.

Table 1. Comparative analysis of unimodal network fusion effects for survival analysis and tumor grading. The two versions of M^2F represent the network with different main task.

Model	Modality	C-index	Acc	AUC	F1-score
CNN	Pathology	0.7385	0.7537	0.8757	0.7047
SNN	Genomics	0.7979	0.6677	0.8567	0.6956
SCNN [17]	Pathology	0.741	–	–	–
GSCNN [17]	Multi-modal	0.781	–	–	–
DOF [2]	Multi-modal	0.788	–	–	–
MMD [6]	Multi-modal	0.8053	–	–	–
MCAT [5]	Multi-modal	0.817	–	–	–
Pathomic Fusion [4]	Multi-modal	0.7994	0.7557	0.8906	0.7239
M^2F-A (Ours)	Multi-modal	**0.8266**	0.6642	0.8516	0.7086
M^2F-B (Ours)	Multi-modal	0.7639	**0.7613**	**0.8919**	**0.7322**

As shown in the Table 1, multi-modal networks generally show better performance than unimodal networks in both diagnosis and prognosis. It is worth noting that we only reproduce Pathomic Fusion because of limited codes and there have some differences in experimental details. DOF [2] and MMD [6] are

Table 2. Comparative analysis of single-task learning and multi-task learning. The task font in bold means the main task.

Tasks	TMG	C-index	Acc	AUC	F1-score
Surv		0.8066	–	–	–
Grad		–	0.7569	0.8891	0.7256
Surv&Grad		0.8188	0.6753	0.8550	0.7097
Surv&**Grad**		0.7639	**0.7613**	0.8919	**0.7322**
Surv&Grad	✓	**0.8266**	0.6642	0.8516	0.7086
Surv&**Grad**	✓	0.7816	0.7576	**0.8930**	0.7276

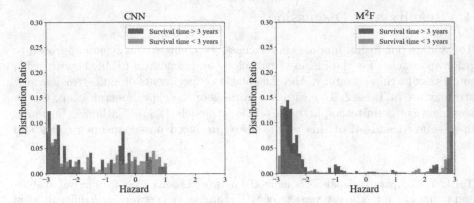

Fig. 3. The distribution of networks prediction hazard. Patients with long survival time (blue) represent that they have lower risks in this moment and red means they have short survival time at higher risk. Compared to unimodal CNN, our M^2F is observed to be able to stratify different patients better. (Color figure online)

both using four modalities with additional radiology and clinical information. Besides, MCAT [5] uses WSIs for training. Despite this, our M^2F outperforms other previous models in both survival analysis task and tumor grading task, which has achieved improvement in all evaluation metrics. The results of Table 1 demonstrate that our M^2F can interact multi-modal features well and learn the correlation and complementary information of different modalities.

In order to validate our multi-task strategy, we compare the difference in performance between single-task training and joint training by conducting ablation

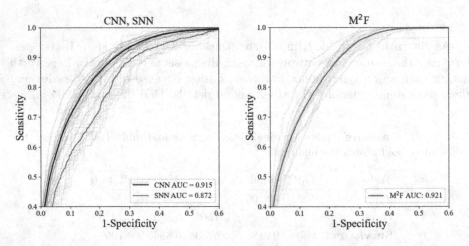

Fig. 4. The receiver operating characteristic curve (ROC) of tumor grading task. These two represent the ROC curves of the single-modal network and the multi-modal network, respectively.

experiments. For multi-task learning without TMG, we train two MLP heads in parallel for both tasks and there is no connection between the two heads. As shown in Table 2, jointly training survival task and grading task utilize the complementarity between tasks. In the Table 2, the multi-task learning strategy helps our model improve performance, this results demonstrate the advantages of multi-task learning over single-task learning. The addition of TMG further improves model performance at survival analysis task which once more demonstrates the effectiveness of multi-task learning.

5   Conclusion

In this paper, we present M²F, a efficient framework for novel fusion of modalities and integrating survival analysis task and tumor grading task for model the correlation between multiple tasks. The co-attention mechanism which is the core of MTE show the ability to implement modal interaction and our TMG module demonstrate strong potential in the field of multi-task learning. We validate our approach on glioma dataset and demonstrate that our MTE and TMG module can respectively act as a effective tool for multi-modal learning and multi-task learning. Moreover, our M²F can be applied to any cancers for diagnosis, prognosis, and any other tasks.

Acknowledgement. This work was supported in part by the Natural Science Foundation of Ningbo City, China, under Grant 2021J052, in part by the National Natural Science Foundation of China under Grants 62171377, and in part by the Key Research and Development Program of Shaanxi Province under Grant 2022GY-084.

References

1. Baltrušaitis, T., Ahuja, C., Morency, L.P.: Multimodal machine learning: a survey and taxonomy. IEEE Trans. Pattern Anal. Mach. Intell. **41**(2), 423–443 (2018)
2. Braman, N., Gordon, J.W.H., Goossens, E.T., Willis, C., Stumpe, M.C., Venkataraman, J.: Deep orthogonal fusion: multimodal prognostic biomarker discovery integrating radiology, pathology, genomic, and clinical data. In: de Bruijne, M., Cattin, P.C., Cotin, S., Padoy, N., Speidel, S., Zheng, Y., Essert, C. (eds.) MICCAI 2021. LNCS, vol. 12905, pp. 667–677. Springer, Cham (2021). https://doi.org/10.1007/978-3-030-87240-3_64
3. Cerami, E., et al.: The cbio cancer genomics portal: an open platform for exploring multidimensional cancer genomics data. Cancer Discov. **2**(5), 401–404 (2012)
4. Chen, R.J., et al.: Pathomic fusion: an integrated framework for fusing histopathology and genomic features for cancer diagnosis and prognosis. IEEE Trans. Med. Imaging **41**(4), 757–770 (2020)
5. Chen, R.J., et al.: Multimodal co-attention transformer for survival prediction in gigapixel whole slide images. In: Proceedings of the IEEE/CVF International Conference on Computer Vision, pp. 4015–4025 (2021)
6. Cui, C., et al.: Survival prediction of brain cancer with incomplete radiology, pathology, genomics, and demographic data. arXiv preprint. arXiv:2203.04419 (2022)

7. Gallego, O.: Nonsurgical treatment of recurrent glioblastoma. Curr. Oncol. **22**(4), 273–281 (2015)
8. Gurcan, M.N., Boucheron, L.E., Can, A., Madabhushi, A., Rajpoot, N.M., Yener, B.: Histopathological image analysis: a review. IEEE Rev. Biomed. Eng. **2**, 147–171 (2009)
9. He, K., Zhang, X., Ren, S., Sun, J.: Deep residual learning for image recognition. In: Proceedings of the IEEE/CVF International Conference on Computer Vision, pp. 770–778 (2016)
10. Kang, M., Ko, E., Mersha, T.B.: A roadmap for multi-omics data integration using deep learning. Briefings Bioinformatics **23**(1), bbab454 (2022)
11. Katzman, J.L., Shaham, U., Cloninger, A., Bates, J., Jiang, T., Kluger, Y.: Deep-surv: personalized treatment recommender system using a cox proportional hazards deep neural network. BMC Med. Res. Methodol. **18**(1), 1–12 (2018)
12. Kim, J.H., Jun, J., Zhang, B.T.: Bilinear attention networks. In: Advances in Neural Information Processing Systems, vol. 31 (2018)
13. Kim, W., Son, B., Kim, I.: Vilt: Vision-and-language transformer without convolution or region supervision. In: International Conference on Machine Learning, pp. 5583–5594. PMLR (2021)
14. Klambauer, G., Unterthiner, T., Mayr, A., Hochreiter, S.: Self-normalizing neural networks. In: Advances in Neural Information Processing Systems, vol. 30 (2017)
15. Louis, D.N., et al.: The 2021 who classification of tumors of the central nervous system: a summary. Neuro Oncol. **23**(8), 1231–1251 (2021)
16. Lu, J., Yang, J., Batra, D., Parikh, D.: Hierarchical question-image co-attention for visual question answering. In: Advances in Neural Information Processing Systems, vol. 29 (2016)
17. Mobadersany, P., et al.: Predicting cancer outcomes from histology and genomics using convolutional networks. Proc. Natl. Acad. Sci. **115**(13), E2970–E2979 (2018)
18. Ngiam, J., Khosla, A., Kim, M., Nam, J., Lee, H., Ng, A.Y.: Multimodal deep learning. In: International Conference on Machine Learning (2011)
19. Simonyan, K., Zisserman, A.: Very deep convolutional networks for large-scale image recognition. arXiv preprint. arXiv:1409.1556 (2014)
20. Sun, X., Panda, R., Feris, R., Saenko, K.: Adashare: learning what to share for efficient deep multi-task learning. Adv. Neural. Inf. Process. Syst. **33**, 8728–8740 (2020)
21. Vafaeikia, P., Wagner, M.W., Tabori, U., Ertl-Wagner, B.B., Khalvati, F.: Improving the segmentation of pediatric low-grade gliomas through multitask learning. arXiv preprint. arXiv:2111.14959 (2021)
22. Vandenhende, S., Georgoulis, S., Van Gansbeke, W., Proesmans, M., Dai, D., Van Gool, L.: Multi-task learning for dense prediction tasks: a survey. IEEE Trans. Pattern Anal. Mach. Intell. **44**(7), 3614–3633 (2021)
23. Vaswani, A., et al.: Attention is all you need. In: Advances in Neural Information Processing Systems, vol. 30 (2017)
24. Wang, P., Li, Y., Reddy, C.K.: Machine learning for survival analysis: a survey. ACM Comput. Surv. (CSUR) **51**(6), 1–36 (2019)
25. Wang, R., Huang, Z., Wang, H., Wu, H.: Ammasurv: asymmetrical multi-modal attention for accurate survival analysis with whole slide images and gene expression data. In: 2021 IEEE International Conference on Bioinformatics and Biomedicine (BIBM), pp. 757–760. IEEE (2021)
26. Wen, P.Y., Reardon, D.A.: Progress in glioma diagnosis, classification and treatment. Nat. Rev. Neurol. **12**(2), 69–70 (2016)

Visual Modalities Based Multimodal Fusion for Surgical Phase Recognition

Bogyu Park[1], Hyeongyu Chi[1], Bokyung Park[1], Jiwon Lee[1], Sunghyun Park[2], Woo Jin Hyung[1,2], and Min-Kook Choi[1(✉)]

[1] Vision AI, Hutom, Seoul, Republic of Korea
{bgpark,hyeongyuc96,bokyung,jiwon,wjhyung,mkchoi}@hutom.io
[2] Yonsei University College of Medicine, Seoul, Republic of Korea
{GODON,wjhyung}@yush.ac

Abstract. We propose visual modalities-based multimodal fusion for surgical phase recognition to overcome the limitation of the diversity of information such as the presence of tools. Through the proposed methods, we extracted a visual kinematics-based index related to the usage of tools such as movement and the relation between tools in surgery. In addition, we improved recognition performance using the effective fusion method which is fusing CNN-based visual feature and visual kinematics-based index. The visual kinematics-based index is helpful for understanding the surgical procedure as the information related to the interaction between tools. Furthermore, these indices can be extracted in any environment unlike kinematics in robotic surgery. The proposed methodology was applied to two multimodal datasets to verify that it can help to improve recognition performance in clinical environments.

Keywords: Surgical workflow · Surgical phase recognition · Multimodal learning · Visual kinematics-based index

1 Introduction

Surgical workflow analysis using a computer-assisted intervention (CAI) system based on machine learning or deep learning has been extensively studied [1–10]. In particular, surgical phase recognition can help optimize surgery by activating communication between surgeons and staffs, not only for smooth teamwork, but also for efficient use of resources throughout the entire surgical procedure [11]. Moreover, it is valuable for monitoring the patient after surgery and educational materials through the classification of stereotyped surgical procedures [1]. However, phase recognition is a challenging task that involves many interactions between the actions of the tools and the organs. In addition, surgical video analysis has limitations such as video quality (i.e. occlusion and illumination change) and unclear annotations at event boundaries [2,3].

Many studies that performed surgical workflow analysis have limitations due to performing analysis using only CNN-based visual features and information

X. Li et al. (Eds.): MMMI 2022, LNCS 13594, pp. 11–23, 2022.
https://doi.org/10.1007/978-3-031-18814-5_2

for the presence of tools in video. In this paper, to overcome this limitation, we introduce a visual modality-based multimodal fusion method that improves the performance of phase recognition by using interactions between the recognized tools. The proposed method extracts indices related to tools used in surgery and fuses them with visual features extracted from CNN. We demonstrate the effectiveness of proposed tool-related indices to improve performance by the VR simulator-based dataset and the collected gastrectomy dataset.

We have the following contributions:

- We propose a method to extract a visual kinematics-based index related to tools that are helpful in surgical workflow analysis from visual modality such as semantic segmentation map.
- In addition, it shows that it can be applied in environments where it is difficult to extract the kinematics of tools in a system unlike robotic surgery.
- We propose a fusion method that improves recognition performance by effectively aggregating the visual kinematics-based index and visual features.

2   Related Works

Phase Recognition. In early machine learning-based research, a statistical analysis of temporal information using Hidden Markov Models (HMMs) and Dynamic Time Warping (DTW) was conducted [4]. Since then, as the use of deep learning has become more active, EndoNet [5] that recognizes tool existence through CNN-based feature extraction had been studied. MTRCNet-CL [6], which combines CNN and LSTM to perform multi-tasks, was also performed. Furthermore, a multi-stage TCN (MS-TCN)-based surgical workflow analysis study that performs hierarchically processes using temporal convolution was also performed [10]. Each stage was designed to refine the values predicted by the previous stage to return more accurate predictions. Previous studies had been conducted using only video information for analysis or additionally using only the presence of tools in the video. On the other hand, the proposed method uses a method of fusing visual features and indices related to tools.

Surgical Workflow Dataset. Datasets published to perform surgical workflow recognition include actual surgical videos like Cholec80 [5], toy samples for action recognition of a simple level such as JIGSAWS [12] and MISAW [13], and synthetic data generated from VR simulators PETRAW [14]. In the case of the JIGSAWS and MISAW, kinematic information of the instrument from the master-slave robotic platform was provided, so that more precise tool movements could be analyzed. However, in laparoscopic surgery, it was difficult to use kinematic information owing to the absence of a surgery robot. There was a limit to extracting and applying actual kinematic information due to security issues of the robotic surgery device. To address these problems, we use a method of generating tool-related indices from visual modality to replace kinematic information.

Multimodal Learning. The various modalities (i.e., video, kinematics) created in the surgical environment have different information about the surgical

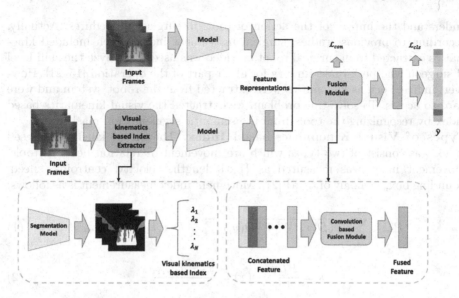

Fig. 1. Proposed visual modalities-based multimodal fusion method. The visual kinematics-based index and frame sequence extracted for the input frame sequence is used as input to the models for each modality. The feature representations of each modality are used as input to the fusion model for joint training.

workflow. Multimodal learning aims to improve performance by using mutual information between each modality. However, researches on multimodal learning in surgical workflow analysis were still insufficient [5,12–15]. In particular, there was a limitation because of related to data that is difficult to access or extract such as the kinematics of surgical tools. We propose a method to effectively achieve performance improvement by fusing various information generated from vision modalities through virtual or real data.

3   Methods

In this section, we propose an extraction manner of a visual kinematics-based index and a visual modality-based multimodal feature fusion method. We used two visual modalities: video and visual kinematics-based index. The visual kinematics-based index expresses the movement and relationship of surgical tools extracted from the semantic segmentation mask. To improve the phase recognition performance, we applied convolutional feature fusion to enhance the interaction of features extracted from visual modalities. The overall learning structure is shown in Fig. 1.

3.1   Visual Kinematics-based Index

A visual kinematics-based index was defined as an index expressing the relationship between tools and the movement of tools. These indices helped to understand the impact of the action of tools in surgical procedures. Actually, according to previous studies, surgical instrument index which included kinematics extracted from surgical robot or video was used to analyze the skill level of surgeon who performed surgery for all or part of the operation [15–21]. However, indices such as kinematics were extracted from the robot system and were hard to access. To solve this problem, we extracted the visual kinematics-based index by recognizing the tools from the semantic segmentation mask.

Types of Visual Kinematics-based Index. The visual kinematics-based index was consist of two types which are movement or relation between tools. Movement index was measured as {path length, velocity, centroids, speed, bounding box, economy of area} [21]. Movement index measurement is as follows:

$$PL = \sum_{t}^{T} \sqrt{(D(x,t))^2 + (D(y,t))^2}, \quad D(x,t) = x_t - x_{t-1}. \tag{1}$$

$$s = \frac{PL}{T}, \quad v(x) = \frac{x_t - x_{t-\Delta}}{\Delta}. \tag{2}$$

$$EOA = \frac{bw \times bh}{W \times H}. \tag{3}$$

where PL is path length in the current time frame t and T is the time range for computing index. The path length consists of two types which are cumulative path length and partial path length. $D(x,t)$ measures the difference of x coordinate between the previous and current time frame. x and y mean centroids of an object in the frame. Centroids are average positional values for X- and Y-coordinate in the semantic segmentation mask. s is the speed for time range T, and v is the velocity for the direction of X or Y at time interval Δ. bw and bh are the width and height of the bounding box, and W and H are the width and height of the image. Bounding box (BBox) is consist of four values such as top, left, box width, box height (bx, by, bw, bh).

Relation index was measured as {IoU, gIoU, cIoU, dIoU} [21–23]. gIoU, cIoU, and dIoU are modified versions of IoU. The index of IoU family is related to how close two objects are to each other. We considered $\{\lambda_1, ..., \lambda_N\}$ to train phase recognition model by index combination experiments. λ denotes a visual kinematics-based index.

3.2 Feature Fusion

The feature representation for each modality has different information regarding surgical workflow. The representation extracted from the video is related to the overall action in the scene, and the representation extracted from the visual index is related to the detailed movement of each tool. We designed a convolution-based feature fusion module for the interaction of representations to improve recognition performance. For performance comparison, a simple linear feature fusion method and a convolution-based feature fusion method were introduced.

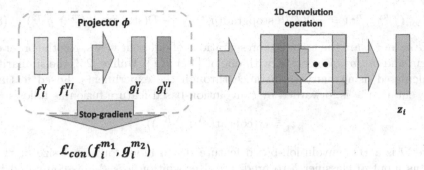

$$\mathcal{L}_{con}(f_i^{m_1}, g_i^{m_2})$$

Fig. 2. An illustration of convolution-based feature fusion module. Before feature fusion, enhancement for feature representation is performed by stop-gradient strategy. After then, features are aggregated by 1D-convolutional operation.

Linear Feature Fusion. For each feature representation from modality, the linear fusion module is as follows:

$$f_i^m = \eta(\theta_m(x_i^m)), \quad m \in \{V, VKI\}. \tag{4}$$

$$z_i = \psi(\text{concat}(f_i^V, f_i^{VKI})). \tag{5}$$

where f_i^m is a d-dimensional projected feature for each modality, x_i^m is ith input data of modality m, and θ_m is a deep neural network based recognition model for each modality. V and VKI denote video and visual kinematics-based index. η and ψ are fusion blocks based on Multi-Layer Perceptron (MLP) layers for generating features of another view and aggregating features, respectively. The concatenated feature is aggregated to d-dimensional feature z_i as the input classification layer.

Convolution Based Feature Fusion. Linear fusion module is not an effective approach due to the simple late-fusion method based on a vanilla fully-connected layer. The proposed convolution-based feature fusion module is effective in enhancing interaction between features for phase recognition. The proposed method is processed in 2 steps; 1) Stop gradient-based representation enhancement, 2) Convolutional feature aggregation as shown in Fig. 2.

$$g_i^m = \phi(f_i^m) \tag{6}$$

We apply the stop gradient-based approach proposed in [24] to close the representations of modality with different views and to speed up the learning convergence speed. g_i^m with the same dimension and different view is generated through a projector composed of MLP in Eq. 6. [24] used contrastive loss to learn similarity between representations. According to [24], the contrastive loss is defined as:

$$\mathcal{D}(a_i, b_i) = (\sum_{j=1}^{d} |a_{i,j} - b_{i,j}|^p)^{1/p} \tag{7}$$

$$\mathcal{L}_{con}(f_i^{m_1}, g_i^{m_2}) = \frac{1}{2}\mathcal{D}(f_i^{m_1}, \text{stopgrad}(g_i^{m_2})) + \frac{1}{2}\mathcal{D}(\text{stopgrad}(f_i^{m_1}), g_i^{m_2}) \quad (8)$$

where a_i and b_i are the feature representations of different views, p is the order of a norm and m_1, m_2 are consist with one of $\{V, VKI\}$. Unlike [24], the similarity is calculated using pairwise distance through the experiments. Fused feature representation z_i is forwarded by convolution-based feature fusion as follows:

$$z_i = \Theta(\text{concat}(g_i^V, g_i^{VKI})) \quad (9)$$

where Θ is a 1D convolution-based feature fusion block for kernel size k, z_i is used as input of classifier h to predict $\hat{y}$. Recognition loss $\mathcal{L}_{cls}$ is computed by cross-entropy loss and then total loss is defined as Eq. 11.

$$\mathcal{L}_{cls} = \text{CrossEntropyLoss}(\hat{y}, y), \quad \hat{y} = h(z_i) \quad (10)$$

$$\mathcal{L}_{total} = \mathcal{L}_{con} + \mathcal{L}_{cls} \quad (11)$$

4 Experiment Results

4.1 Base Setting

Dataset. We validated the proposed methods using two different datasets. 1) PETRAW [14] was released at challenge of MICCAI 2021. PETRAW dataset consisted of the pair which are video, kinematics of arms, and semantic segmentation mask generated from VR simulator. Training and test data were constructed with 90 and 60 pairs, respectively. The PETRAW had four tasks such as Phase(3), Step(13), Left action(7), and Right action(7); values in parentheses are the number of classes. 2) The 40 surgical videos for gastrectomy surgery which is called G40 were collected with da Vinci Si and Xi devices between January 2018 and December 2019. We constructed a 30:10 training and evaluation set by considering the patient's demographic data such as {age, gender, pre_BMI, OP_time, Blood_loss, and length of surgery}. According to [3], G40 dataset was annotated for ARMES based 27 surgical phases by consensus of 3 surgeons. G40 consisted of video and semantic segmentation mask with 31 classes, including tools and organs for {harmonic ace, bipolar forceps, cadiere forceps, grasper, stapler, clip applier, suction irrigation, needle, gauze, specimen bag, drain tube, liver, stomach, pancreas, spleen, and gallbladder}. Each instrument consisted of a head, wrist, and body parts[1].

Model. To train models for various modalities, we used Slowfast50 [25] with α, β, and τ for video and Bi-LSTM [26] for kinematics and visual kinematics based index. The segmentation model was trained to predict semantic segmentation masks for generating an index. We used UperNet [27] with Swin Transformer [28] as backbone network.

---

[1] Please refer supplementary material for class definition details and segmentation results on G40.

Evaluation Metrics. We used various evaluation metrics which are accuracy of whole correctly classified samples, the average version of recall, precision, and F-1 score for classes each task to compare phase recognition results. All metrics were computed frame-by-frame. In all tables, we selected the best models by the average F1 score of tasks.

4.2   Performance Analysis

Table 1. Best combination experiments for visual kinematics based index on PETRAW. $\{\lambda_1, ..., \lambda_N\}$ are indicated in order by cumulative path length(1), partial path length(2), velocity(3), speed(4), EOA(5), centroids(6), IoU(7), gIoU(8), dIoU(9) and cIoU(10). The best combination is selected by mF1-score.

N	Best combination	Phase	Step	Action(L)	Action(R)	Avg.
1	λ_1	88.28	66.68	29.82	29.16	53.48
2	λ_1, λ_2	90.41	67.57	32.62	32.19	55.70
3	$\lambda_1, \lambda_2, \lambda_3$	90.87	68.74	33.12	33.36	56.52
4	$\lambda_1, \lambda_2, \lambda_4, \lambda_6$	90.96	68.85	32.67	33.66	56.53
5	$\lambda_1, \lambda_2, \lambda_3, \lambda_4, \lambda_6$	**91.47**	68.85	**34.18**	**34.03**	**57.13**
6	$\lambda_1, \lambda_2, \lambda_3, \lambda_5, \lambda_8, \lambda_{10}$	89.30	67.77	31.71	32.80	55.40
7	$\lambda_1, \lambda_2, \lambda_3, \lambda_6, \lambda_7, \lambda_8, \lambda_{10}$	89.69	**69.02**	34.06	33.09	56.47
8	except λ_8 and λ_{10}	90.48	68.51	32.74	33.19	56.23
9	except λ_{10}	91.03	68.24	33.04	32.34	56.16
10	ALL	89.90	68.31	33.69	33.31	56.30

Important Feature Selection. We extracted various visual kinematics-based indices, and then what kinds of index pairs are positively affected by performance was evaluated on PETRAW in Table 1. λ_1 and λ_2 were related to performance improvement in all cases, and λ_3 was also significantly affected by performance. Figure 3 shows cumulative counts of the index for each combination of best and worst performance. In best combination, $\{\lambda_1, \lambda_2, \lambda_3, \lambda_6\}$ were mostly used but, λ_6 was also related to achieve worst performance. We used $N = 5$ due to achieve the best performance in that combination. The index of the bounding box was included in all combination experiments because that is influenced by performance improvement in Table 2. The bounding box can be synergy by using other indices because it has the positional information (bx, by) and the information of object size (bw, bh). All indices with a bounding box obtained better performance compared to those not used it.

Performance on PETRAW. We used an Adam optimizer with an initial learning rate of 1e-3, an L2 weight decay of 1e-5, a step scheduler for Bi-LSTM and convolution-based fusion method, and a cosine annealing scheduler with a

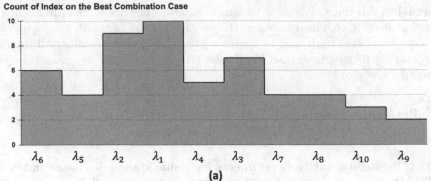

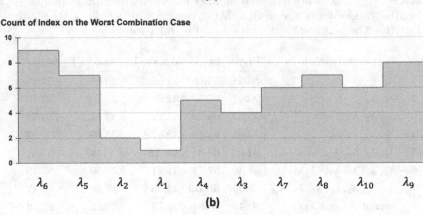

Fig. 3. **The histogram of the visual kinematics-based index for best and worst performance**. (a) Cumulative counts of each index on the combination of best performance (b) Cumulative counts of each index on the combination of worst performance.

warmup scheduler during 34 epochs for slowfast and linear fusion method. A batch size of 128 was used in all experimental environments. The learning rate decay rate was applied at 0.9 every five epochs for step scheduler. According to [25], α, β, and τ were set $\{4, 8, 4\}$ in slowfast. The hidden layer size and output dimension of Bi-LSTM were set at 256 and 256, respectively. Projected feature size d set 512 for both fusion modules, and convolution kernel size k was 3. To address data imbalance, all networks used class-balanced loss [29] and trained for 50 epochs. We also used train and test datasets which were subsampled by 5 fps. The clip size was 8, and the time range T was the same as the clip size.

Table 3 shows mF1 performances for each modality on PETRAW dataset. The baselines, including video and kinematics, were compared to the visual kinematics-based index. Especially, performances of phase and step by visual kinematics based index were achieved similar performance compared to kinematics based performance. It verified that visual kinematics based index can be

Table 2. Evaluation for impact of bounding box. Each row is the performance using a single index. The value in parentheses is the improvement in adding the bounding box, and the bold is the most significant improvement.

Index	Phase	Step	Action(L)	Action(R)	Avg.
BBox only	55.63	27.75	19.57	20.16	30.78
λ_1	83.98(+4.30)	61.37(+5.31)	**9.99(+19.82)**	**10.19(+18.97)**	41.38(+12.10)
λ_2	42.68(+16.84)	14.82(+15.10)	16.32(+9.02)	14.26(+10.74)	22.02(+12.93)
λ_3	**35.88(+22.95)**	13.47(+16.08)	14.78(+8.73)	13.67(+10.07)	19.45(+14.46)
λ_4	35.88(+21.61)	8.75(+20.51)	11.87(+10.95)	10.29(+12.30)	**16.70(+16.34)**
λ_5	36.63(+19.91)	15.38(+13.76)	14.32(+7.91)	14.17(+7.56)	20.13(+12.29)
λ_6	48.58(+6.77)	20.83(+6.59)	17.80(+2.61)	18.11(+3.33)	26.33(+4.82)
λ_7	34.55(+20.75)	7.59(+19.99)	10.16(+10.56)	10.17(+10.54)	15.62(+15.46)
λ_8	34.54(+20.58)	7.18(+20.38)	10.01(+11.01)	10.16(+10.92)	15.47(+15.72)
λ_9	34.22(+21.39)	**6.82(+20.68)**	10.18(+9.98)	10.15(+11.83)	15.34(+15.97)
λ_{10}	33.80(+21.14)	7.10(+20.10)	10.06(+12.02)	10.16(+11.59)	15.28(+16.21)

helpful to recognize the actions of tools in Tables 1, 2, and 3[2]. Furthermore, the proposed fusion technique achieved improved performance compared to baseline. Our fusion methodology was useful for fusing the representations by enhancing the interactions between features.

Performance on G40. As like setting of PETRAW, we used the same setting of training models. However, the initial learning rate was set 1e-2, weighted cross-entropy loss was used for slowfast, and a cosine annealing scheduler was used for all experiments. A batch size of 64 was used in all experimental environments, and all networks were trained for 50 epochs. The sampling rate was set 1 fps for train and test datasets. The clip size was 32, and the time range T was the same as the clip size. It also improved performance by using the visual kinematics-based index on G40 in Table 4. That is, the visual kinematics-based index was available to replace the kinematics in actual surgery.

Table 3. Performance change for each modality on PETRAW. {V, K, VKI} denote video, kinematics and visual kinematics based index.

Model	Modality	Phase	Step	Action(L)	Action(R)	Avg.
Slowfast50	V	98.13	96.15	79.52	78.72	88.13
Bi-LSTM	K	96.79	80.52	78.10	77.01	83.11
Bi-LSTM	VKI	91.47	68.85	34.18	34.03	57.13
Linear Fusion	V+K	98.26	96.13	80.45	**81.86**	86.14
Conv. Fusion	V+K	**98.59**	**96.43**	**82.57**	81.83	**89.85**
Linear Fusion	V+VKI	98.21	96.28	79.93	79.17	85.12
Conv. Fusion	V+VKI	98.23	96.38	79.87	78.98	88.36

---

[2] Please refer to supplementary material for additional experimental results of Accuracy, mPrecision, mRecall, and mF1 on PETRAW.

Table 4. Performance change of each modality on G40. mPrecision, mRecall, and mF1 are measured by the average of results for each class.

Model	Modality	Accuracy	mPrecision	mRecall	mF1
Slowfast50	V	63.37	55.40	59.10	55.49
Bi-LSTM	VKI	50.53	40.32	36.79	34.80
Linear Fusion	V+VKI	**69.71**	56.58	58.83	56.76
Conv. Fusion	V+VKI	67.71	**56.75**	**60.19**	**57.41**

4.3   Ablation Study

Visual Kinematics Based Index for Organs. The surgical procedure was related to the interaction between tools and organs. Therefore, relation indices of tools and organs can be helped for recognition performance. We evaluated the performance change by involving a relation index between tools and organs. We used λ_8 and λ_{10} measured between tools and organs for considering the relationship. The comparison is shown in Table 5. Those indices were validated to help recognize the surgical procedure by improved performance.

Table 5. The comparative results for including indices of organs on G40. We compared by adding the relation index between tools and organs, including the liver, stomach, pancreas, spleen, and gallbladder.

Model	Index	Accuracy	mPrecision	mRecall	mF1
Bi-LSTM	tools only	52.58	41.40	40.76	39.46
Bi-LSTM	add organs	**53.72**	**44.04**	**41.10**	**40.67**

Change of Semantic Model. We evaluated the change in performance regarding segmentation models. We considered three models, DeeplabV3+ [30], UperNet [27], and OCRNet [31]. UperNet used Swin Transformer [28] as backbone network and HRNet [32] for OCRNet. We used the basic setting of MMSegmentation [33] to train models during 100 and 300 epochs on PETRAW and G40, respectively. According to accurate segmentation results, the performance was improved in Table 6.

Table 6. Performance change for various segmentation models on PETRAW. The values in table are mF1-score for each task.

Seg. Model	Target Model	mIoU	Phase	Step	Action(L)	Action(R)	Avg.
DeeplabV3+	Bi-LSTM	**98.99**	89.91	61.83	24.33	22.40	49.62
OCR-HRNet	Bi-LSTM	98.98	**92.06**	68.67	31.71	**35.02**	56.86
Swin-UperNet	Bi-LSTM	98.94	91.47	68.85	**34.18**	34.03	**57.13**

Table 7. Performance change for various segmentation models on G40.

Seg. Model	Target Model	mIoU	Accuracy	mPrecision	mRecall	mF1
DeeplabV3+	Bi-LSTM	85.14	50.20	39.96	37.58	36.69
OCR-HRNet	Bi-LSTM	86.45	50.40	39.66	40.30	38.39
Swin-UperNet	Bi-LSTM	**87.64**	**52.58**	**41.40**	**40.76**	**39.46**

5 Conclusion

We proposed a visual modalities-based feature fusion method for recognizing surgical procedures. We extracted a visual kinematics-based index from a visual modality such as a semantic segmentation map and trained the model using the indices and visual features from CNN. We validated that our approach helped to recognize the surgical procedure in simple simulation (PETRAW) and actual surgery (G40). In addition, the visual kinematics-based index is expected to be helpful in non-robotic surgery like laparoscopic surgery due to generating them from visual modality. For further study, we will consider evaluating by extracting a visual kinematics-based index from other visual modalities such as the object detection model.

Acknowledgement. "This research was funded by the Ministry of Health & Welfare, Republic of Korea (grant number : 1465035498 / HI21C1753000022)."

References

1. Zisimopoulos, O., et al.: DeepPhase: surgical phase recognition in CATARACTS Videos. In: Frangi, A.F., Schnabel, J.A., Davatzikos, C., Alberola-López, C., Fichtinger, G. (eds.) MICCAI 2018. LNCS, vol. 11073, pp. 265–272. Springer, Cham (2018). https://doi.org/10.1007/978-3-030-00937-3_31
2. Klank, U., Padoy, N., Feussner, H., Navab, N.: Automatic feature generation in endoscopic images. Int. J. Comput. Assist. Radiol. Surg. 3(3), 331–339 (2008). https://doi.org/10.1007/s11548-008-0223-8
3. Hong, S., et al.: Rethinking generalization performance of surgical phase recognition with expert-generated annotations. arXiv preprint. arXiv:2110.11626 (2021)
4. Padoy, N., Blum, T., Ahmadi, S.-A., Feussner, H., Berger, M.-O., Navab, N.: Statistical modeling and recognition of surgical workflow. Med. Image Anal. 16(3), 632–641 (2012)

5. Twinanda, A.P., Shehata, S., Mutter, D., Marescaux, J., De Mathelin, M., Padoy, N.: Endonet: a deep architecture for recognition tasks on laparoscopic videos. IEEE Trans. Med. Imaging **36**(1), 86–97 (2016)
6. Jin, Y.: Multi-task recurrent convolutional network with correlation loss for surgical video analysis. Med. Image Anal. **59**, 101572 (2020)
7. Lecuyer, G., Ragot, M., Martin, N., Launay, L., Jannin, P.: Assisted phase and step annotation for surgical videos. Int. J. Comput. Assist. Radiol. Surg. **15**(4), 673–680 (2020). https://doi.org/10.1007/s11548-019-02108-8
8. Dergachyova, O., Bouget, D., Huaulmé, A., Morandi, X., Jannin, P.: Automatic data-driven real-time segmentation and recognition of surgical workflow. Int. J. Comput. Assist. Radiol. Surg. **11**(6), 1081–1089 (2016). https://doi.org/10.1007/s11548-016-1371-x
9. Loukas, C.: Video content analysis of surgical procedures. Surg. Endosc. **32**(2), 553–568 (2017). https://doi.org/10.1007/s00464-017-5878-1
10. Czempiel, T., et al.: TeCNO: surgical phase recognition with multi-stage temporal convolutional networks. In: Martel, A.L., et al. (eds.) MICCAI 2020. LNCS, vol. 12263, pp. 343–352. Springer, Cham (2020). https://doi.org/10.1007/978-3-030-59716-0_33
11. Maier-Hein, L., et al.: Surgical data science for next-generation interventions. Nat. Biomed. Eng. **1**(9), 691–696 (2017)
12. Gao, Y., et al.: Jhu-isi gesture and skill assessment working set (jigsaws): a surgical activity dataset for human motion modeling. In: MICCAI Workshop: M2cai, vol. 3 (2014)
13. Huaulmé, A., et al.: Micro-surgical anastomose workflow recognition challenge report. Comput. Methods Programs Biomed. **212**, 106452 (2021)
14. Huaulmé, A., et al.: Peg transfer workflow recognition challenge report: does multi-modal data improve recognition? arXiv preprint. arXiv:2202.05821 (2022)
15. Khalid, S., Goldenberg, M., Grantcharov, T., Taati, B., Rudzicz, F.: Evaluation of deep learning models for identifying surgical actions and measuring performance. JAMA Netw. Open **3**(3), e201664–e201664 (2020)
16. Funke, I., Mees, S.T., Weitz, J., Speidel, S.: Video-based surgical skill assessment using 3D convolutional neural networks. Int. J. Comput. Assist. Radiol. Surg. **14**(7), 1217–1225 (2019). https://doi.org/10.1007/s11548-019-01995-1
17. Hung, A.J., Chen, J., Jarc, A., Hatcher, D., Djaladat, H., Gill, I.S.: Development and validation of objective performance metrics for robot-assisted radical prostatectomy: a pilot study. J. Urol. **199**(1), 296–304 (2018)
18. Lee, D., Yu, H.W., Kwon, H., Kong, H.J., Lee, K.E., Kim, H.C.: Evaluation of surgical skills during robotic surgery by deep learning-based multiple surgical instrument tracking in training and actual operations. J. Clin. Med. **9**(6), 1964 (2020)
19. Liu, D., et al.: Towards unified surgical skill assessment. In: Proceedings of the IEEE/CVF Conference on Computer Vision and Pattern Recognition, pp. 9522–9531 (2021)
20. Birkmeyer, J.D., et al.: Surgical skill and complication rates after bariatric surgery. N. Engl. J. Med. **369**(15), 1434–1442 (2013)
21. Oropesa, I., et al.: Eva: laparoscopic instrument tracking based on endoscopic video analysis for psychomotor skills assessment. Surg. Endosc. **27**(3), 1029–1039 (2013). https://doi.org/10.1007/s00464-012-2513-z
22. Rezatofighi, H., Tsoi, N., Gwak, J., Sadeghian, A., Reid, I., Savarese, S.: Generalized intersection over union: a metric and a loss for bounding box regression. In: Proceedings of the IEEE/CVF Conference on Computer Vision and Pattern Recognition, pp. 658–666 (2019)

23. Zheng, Z., Wang, P., Liu, W., Li, J., Ye, R., Ren, D.: Distance-iou loss: Faster and better learning for bounding box regression. In: Proceedings of the AAAI Conference on Artificial Intelligence **34**, 12993–13000 (2020)

24. Chen, X., He, K.: Exploring simple siamese representation learning. In: Proceedings of the IEEE/CVF Conference on Computer Vision and Pattern Recognition, pp. 15750–15758 (2021)

25. Feichtenhofer, C., Fan, H., Malik, J., He, K.: Slowfast networks for video recognition. In: Proceedings of the IEEE/CVF International Conference on Computer Vision, pp. 6202–6211 (2019)

26. Schuster, M., Paliwal, K.K.: Bidirectional recurrent neural networks. IEEE Trans. Sig. Process. **45**(11), 2673–2681 (1997)

27. Xiao, T., Liu, Y., Zhou, B., Jiang, Y., Sun, J.: Unified perceptual parsing for scene understanding. In: Proceedings of the European Conference on Computer Vision (ECCV), pp. 418–434 (2018)

28. Liu, Z., et al.: Swin transformer: hierarchical vision transformer using shifted windows. In: Proceedings of the IEEE/CVF International Conference on Computer Vision, pp. 10012–10022 (2021)

29. Cui, Y., Jia, M., Lin, T.Y., Song, Y., Belongie, S.: Class-balanced loss based on effective number of samples. In: Proceedings of the IEEE/CVF Conference on Computer Vision and Pattern Recognition, pp. 9268–9277 (2019)

30. Chen, L.C., Zhu, Y., Papandreou, G., Schroff, F., Adam, H.: Encoder-decoder with atrous separable convolution for semantic image segmentation. In: Proceedings of the European Conference on Computer Vision (ECCV), pp. 801–818 (2018)

31. Yuan, Y., Chen, X., Wang, J.: Object-contextual representations for semantic segmentation. In: Vedaldi, A., Bischof, H., Brox, T., Frahm, J.-M. (eds.) ECCV 2020. LNCS, vol. 12351, pp. 173–190. Springer, Cham (2020). https://doi.org/10.1007/978-3-030-58539-6_11

32. Sun, K., Xiao, B., Liu, D., Wang, J.: Deep high-resolution representation learning for human pose estimation. In: Proceedings of the IEEE/CVF Conference on Computer Vision and Pattern Recognition, pp. 5693–5703 (2019)

33. MMSegmentation Contributors. MMSegmentation: Openmmlab semantic segmentation toolbox and benchmark. https://github.com/open-mmlab/mmsegmentation (2020)

Cross-Scale Attention Guided Multi-instance Learning for Crohn's Disease Diagnosis with Pathological Images

Ruining Deng[1], Can Cui[1], Lucas W. Remedios[1], Shunxing Bao[1],
R. Michael Womick[2], Sophie Chiron[3], Jia Li[3], Joseph T. Roland[3], Ken S. Lau[1],
Qi Liu[3], Keith T. Wilson[3,4], Yaohong Wang[3], Lori A. Coburn[3,4],
Bennett A. Landman[1], and Yuankai Huo[1(✉)]

[1] Vanderbilt University, Nashville, TN 37215, USA
yuankai.huo@vanderbilt.edu
[2] The University of North Carolina at Chapel Hill, Chapel Hill, NC 27514, USA
[3] Vanderbilt University Medical Center, Nashville, TN 37232, USA
[4] Veterans Affairs Tennessee Valley Healthcare System, Nashville, TN 37212, USA

Abstract. Multi-instance learning (MIL) is widely used in the computer-aided interpretation of pathological Whole Slide Images (WSIs) to solve the lack of pixel-wise or patch-wise annotations. Often, this approach directly applies "natural image driven" MIL algorithms which overlook the multi-scale (i.e. pyramidal) nature of WSIs. Off-the-shelf MIL algorithms are typically deployed on a single-scale of WSIs (e.g., 20× magnification), while human pathologists usually aggregate the global and local patterns in a multi-scale manner (e.g., by zooming in and out between different magnifications). In this study, we propose a novel cross-scale attention mechanism to explicitly aggregate inter-scale interactions into a single MIL network for Crohn's Disease (CD), which is a form of inflammatory bowel disease. The contribution of this paper is two-fold: (1) a cross-scale attention mechanism is proposed to aggregate features from different resolutions with multi-scale interaction; and (2) differential multi-scale attention visualizations are generated to localize explainable lesion patterns. By training ∼250,000 H&E-stained Ascending Colon (AC) patches from 20 CD patient and 30 healthy control samples at different scales, our approach achieved a superior Area under the Curve (AUC) score of 0.8924 compared with baseline models. The official implementation is publicly available at https://github.com/hrlblab/CS-MIL.

Keywords: Multi-instance Learning · Multi-scale · Attention mechanism · Pathology

1 Introduction

Digital pathology is relied upon heavily by clinicians to accurately diagnose Crohn's Disease (CD) [14,32]. Pathologists carefully examine biopsies at multiple scales through microscopes to examine morphological patterns [6], which is a laborious task.

X. Li et al. (Eds.): MMMI 2022, LNCS 13594, pp. 24–33, 2022.
https://doi.org/10.1007/978-3-031-18814-5_3

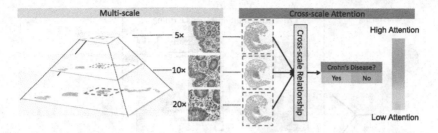

Fig. 1. Multi-scale awareness. Human pathologists typically aggregate the global and local patterns in a multi-scale manner. However, previous work failed to be aware of cross-scale relationship at different resolutions. Our method demonstrates the importance-of-regions with cross-scale attention maps, and aggregate the multi-scale patterns with differential attention scores for CD diagnosis.

With the rapid development of whole slide imaging (WSI) and deep learning methods, computer-assisted CD clinical prediction and exploration [9,18,19,27] are increasingly promising endeavors. However, annotating images pixel- or patch-wise is computationally expensive for a standard supervised learning system [11,16,23,24]. To achieve accurate diagnoses from weakly annotated images (e.g., patient-wise diagnosis), multi-instance Learning (MIL) – a widely used weakly supervised learning paradigm – has been applied to digital pathology [7,21,22,26,29]. For example, DeepAttnMISL [31] clustered image patches into different "bags" to model and aggregate diverse local features for patient-level diagnosis.

However, most prior efforts, especially the "natural image driven" MIL algorithms, ignore the multi-scale (i.e., pyramidal) nature of WSIs. For example, a WSI consists of a hierarchical scales of images (from $40\times$ to $5\times$), which allows pathologists to examine both local [2] and global [1] morphological features [5,13,28]. More recent efforts have mimicked such human pathological assessments by using multi-scale images in a WSI [15,20]. These methods typically perform independent feature extraction at each scale and then perform a "late fusion". In this study, we consider the feasibility of examining the interaction between different scales at an earlier stage through an attention-based "early fusion" paradigm.

In this paper, we propose the addition of a novel cross-scale attention mechanism in an attention-guided MIL scheme to explicitly model inter-scale interactions during feature extraction (Fig. 1). In summary, the proposed method not only utilizes the morphological features at different scales (with different fields of view), but also learns their inter-scale interactions as a "early fusion" learning paradigm. Through empirical validation, our approach achieved the higher Area under the Curve (AUC) scores, Average Precision (AP) scores, and classification accuracy. The contribution of this paper is two-fold:

- A novel cross-scale attention mechanism is proposed to integrate the multi-scale information and the inter-scale relationships.
- Differential cross-scale attention visualizations are generated for lesion pattern guidance and exploration.

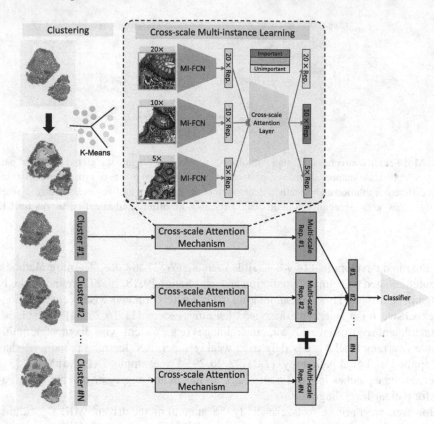

Fig. 2. Cross-scale Attention Guided Multi-instance Learning Pipeline. This figure demonstrates the pipeline of the proposed method. The local feature-based clustering was deployed on each WSI to distribute the phenotype patterns in each MIL bag. The cross-scale attention mechanism is deployed in each cluster of MIL branch to combine the multi-scale features with differential attention scores. Multi-scale representations from different clusters were concatenated for CD classification.

2   Methods

The overall pipeline of the proposed CS-MIL is presented in Fig. 2. Patches at each location (same center coordinates) at different scales are jointly tiled from WSIs. Patch-wise phenotype features are extracted from a self-supervised model. Then, local feature-based clustering is deployed on each WSI to distribute the phenotype patterns in each MIL bag. Cross-scale attention-guided MIL is proposed to aggregate features in multi-scale and multi-clustered settings. A cross-scale attention map is generated for human visual examination.

2.1   Feature Embedding and Phenotype Clustering

In the MIL community, most histopathological image analysis methods are divided into two stages [10,25]: (1) the self-supervised feature embedding stage and (2) the weakly supervised feature-based learning stage. We follow a similar design that leverages our dataset to train a contrastive-learning model SimSiam [8] to extract high-level phenotype features from patches. All of the patches are then embedded into low-dimensional feature vectors for the classification in the second stage.

Inspired by [31], we implement K-means clustering to cluster patches on the patient level based on their self-supervised embeddings from the first stage since the high-level features are more comprehensive than low-resolution thumbnail images in representing phenotypes [33]. When gathering the patches equally from different clusters, the bag with the better generalization for the MIL model can be organized with distinctive phenotype patterns sparsely distributed on WSIs. In contrast, patches with similar high-level features can be aggregated for classification without spatial limitation.

2.2 Cross-Scale Attention Mechanism

We implement the MI-FCN encoder from DeepAttnMISL [31] as the backbone to encode patch embeddings from corresponding phenotype clusters and aggregate the instance-wise features to the patient-wise classification, which showed superior performance on survival prediction on WSIs. In the MIL community, several attention mechanisms [17,22] have been proposed for instance-relationship between different locations on WSIs. However, those methods are not aware of modeling multi-scale patterns from the pyramid-structured WSIs. Some approaches [15,20] have aggregated multi-scale features into deep learning models from WSIs. Unfortunately, those methods fail to exploit relationships between multiple resolutions at the same location.

To address this issue, we propose a cross-scale attention mechanism to represent distinctive awareness at different scales in the backbone. After separately encoding embedding features at different scales, the cross-scale attention mechanism from those encoding features is leveraged to consider the importance of each scale when aggregating multi-scale features at the same location. These attention scores are multiplied by representations from multiple scales to fuse the cross-scale embedding. The multi-scale representation F can be calculated by:

$$F = \sum_{s=1}^{S} a_s f_s \tag{1}$$

where

$$a_s = \frac{\exp \mathbf{W}^{\mathrm{T}} tanh(\mathbf{V} f_s^{\mathrm{T}})}{\sum_{s=1}^{S} \exp \mathbf{W}^{\mathrm{T}} tanh(\mathbf{V} f_s^{\mathrm{T}})} \tag{2}$$

$\mathbf{W} \in \mathbb{R}^{L \times 1}$ and $\mathbf{V} \in \mathbb{R}^{L \times M}$ are trainable parameters in the cross-scale attention layer. L is the size of the MI-FCN output f_s, M is the output channel of the hidden layer in the cross-scale attention layer. Tangent element-wise non-linearity activation function $tanh(.)$ is implemented both negative and positive values for proper gradient flow. S is the number of the scales on WSIs. The attention-based instance-level pooling operator from [31] is then deployed to achieve patient-wise classification with cross-scale embedding.

2.3   Cross-Scale Attention Visualisation

The cross-scale attention maps from the cross-scale attention mechanism on WSIs are presented to show the distinctive contribution of phenotype features at different scales. The cross-scale attentions are mapped from patch scores of the cross-scale attention mechanism on WSIs, demonstrating the importance at multiple resolutions. This attention maps concatenate scale knowledge and location information can expand clinical clues for disease-guiding and exploration in different contexts.

3   Experiments

3.1   Data

50 H&E-stained Ascending Colon (AC) biopsies from [4], which are representative in CD, were collected from 20 CD patients and 30 healthy controls for training. The stained tissues were scanned at $20\times$ magnification. For the pathological diagnosis, the 20 slides from CD patients were scored as normal, quiescent, mild, moderate, or severe. The remaining tissue slides from healthy controls were scored as normal. 116 AC biopsies were stained and scanned for testing with the same procedure as the above training set. The biopsies were acquired from 72 CD patients who have no overlap with the patients in the training data.

3.2   Experimental Setting

256×256 pixels patches were tiled at three scales ($20\times$, $10\times$ and $5\times$). For $20\times$ patches, each pixel is equal to 0.5 Micron. Three individual models following the official SimSiam with a ResNet-50 backbone were trained at three scales, respectively. All three models were trained in 200 epochs with a batch size of 128 with the official setting. 2048-channel embedding vectors were received for all patches. K-means clustering with a class number of 8 was implemented to receive phenotype clustering within the single-scale features at three resolutions, and multi-scale features that include all resolutions for each patient.

10 data splits were randomly organized following the leave-one-out strategy in the training dataset, while the testing dataset was separated into 10 splits with a balanced class distribution. Each bag for MIL models was collected for each patient, equally selecting from different phenotype clustering classes, marked with a slide-wise label from clinicians. Negative Log-Likelihood Loss (NLLLoss) [30] was used to compare the slide-wise prediction for the bag with the weakly label. The validation loss was used to select the optimal model on each data split, while the mean value of the performance on 10 data splits was evaluated as the testing results. Receiver Operating Characteristic (ROC) curves with Area under the Curve (AUC) scores, Precision-Recall (PR) curves with Average Precision (AP) scores, and classification accuracy were used to estimate the performance of each model. We followed the previous work [12] to implement the bootstrapped two-tailed test and the DeLong test to compare the performance between the different models. The cross-scale attention scores were normalized within every single scale between 0 to 1.

Table 1. Classification performance on testing dataset.

Model	Patch scale	Clustering scale	AUC	AP	Acc
DeepAttnMISL(20×) [31]	Single	20×	0.7961	0.6764	0.7156
DeepAttnMISL(10×) [31]	Single	10×	0.7992	0.7426	0.6897
DeepAttnMISL(5×) [31]	Single	5×	0.8390	0.7481	0.7156
Gated attention [17]	Multiple	Multiple	0.8479	0.7857	0.7500
DeepAttnMISL [31]	Multiple	Multiple	0.8340	0.7701	0.7069
MDMIL-CNN [15]	Multiple	5×	0.8813	0.8584	0.7759
DSMIL [20]	Multiple	5×	0.8759	0.8440	0.7672
CS-MIL(Ours)	Multiple	5×	**0.8924**	**0.8724**	**0.8017**

Table 2. The bootstrapped two-tailed test and the DeLong test between different methods.

Model	p-value of AUC	p-value of AP
DeepAttnMISL(20×) [31]	0.004	0.001
DeepAttnMISL(10×) [31]	0.001	0.002
DeepAttnMISL(5×) [31]	0.048	0.004
Gated attention [17]	0.070	0.031
DeepAttnMISL [31]	0.009	0.002
MDMIL-CNN [15]	0.466	0.457
DSMIL [20]	0.350	0.201
CS-MIL(Ours)	Ref.	Ref.

4   Results

4.1   Performance on Classification

We implemented multiple DeepAttnMISL [31] models with patches at different scales
with a single-scale setting. At the same time, we trained the Gated Attention (GA)
model [17] and DeepAttnMISL model with multi-scale patches, without differentiating
scale information. Patches from multiple scales are treated as instances when processing phenotype clustering and patch selection for MIL bags. Furthermore, we adopted
a multi-scale feature aggregations, jointly adding embedding features from the same
location at different scales into each MIL bag as [15]. We also concatenated embedding features from the same location at different scales as [20]. We followed above
multi-scale aggregation to input phenotype features into the DeepAttnMISL backbone
to evaluate the baseline multi-scale MIL models as well as our proposed method. All
of the models were trained and validated within the same hyper-parameter setting and
data splits.

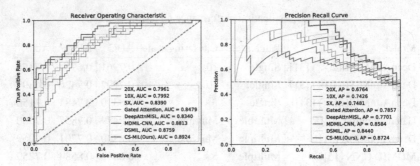

Fig. 3. ROC curves with AUC scores and PR curves with AP scores. This figure shows the ROC curves and PR curves of baseline models as well as the AUC scores and AP scores. The proposed model with cross-scale attention mechanism achieved superior performance in two metrics.

Table 3. Comparison of different cross-scale attention mechanism designs on testing dataset.

Id	Attention layer kernel	Activation function	AUC	AP	Mean of scores
1	Non-sharing	ReLU	0.8575	0.8559	0.8576
2	Non-sharing	Tanh	0.8848	0.8679	0.8763
3*	Sharing	ReLU	**0.8924**	**0.8724**	**0.8824**
4	Sharing	Tanh	0.8838	0.8609	0.8723

Testing Result. Table 1 and Fig. 3 indicates the performance of the performance while directly applying the models on the testing dataset in the CD classification task, without retraining. In general, single-scale models achieved worse performance compared to multi-scale models, indicating the benefit of external knowledge from multiple scale information. The proposed CS-MIL achieved better scores in all evaluation metrics, showing the benefits of the cross-scale attention which explores the inter-scale relationship at different scales in MIL. Table 2 shows the bootstrapped two-tailed test and the DeLong test to compare the performance between the different models.

Cross-Scale Attention Visualisation. Figure 4 represents cross-scale attention maps from the cross-scale attention mechanism on a CD WSI and normal WSI. The proposed CS-MIL can present distinctive importance-of-regions on WSIs at different scales, merging multi-scale and multi-region visualization. As a result, the 20× attention map highlights the chronic inflammatory infiltrates, while the 10× attention map focuses on

Table 4. Comparison of different bag sizes on testing dataset.

Bag size	AUC	AP	Mean of scores
64	0.8507	0.8220	0.8363
16	0.8690	0.8523	0.8606
08*	**0.8924**	**0.8724**	**0.8824**
01	0.8769	0.8261	0.8515

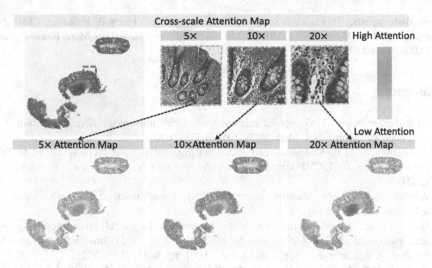

Fig. 4. Attention Map Visualization. This figure shows the cross-scale attention maps from the proposed model. The proposed CS-MIL can present importance-of-regions at different scales.

the crypt structures. Those regions of interest interpret the discriminative regions for CD diagnosis across multiple scales.

4.2 Ablation Studies

Inspired by [31] and [17], we estimated several attention mechanism designs in MIL with different activation functions. We formed the cross-scale attention learning into two strategies, differentiated by whether they shared the kernel weights while learning the embedding features from multiple scales. We also evaluated the performance of different bag sizes. As a result, as shown in Table 3, sharing the kernel weight for cross-scale attention learning with ReLU [3] achieved better performances with a higher mean value of multiple metrics. Table 4 demonstrates that a bag size of 8 is an optimal hyper-parameter for this study. The * is the proposed design.

5   Conclusion

In this work, we propose the addition of a cross-scale attention mechanism to an attention-guided MIL to combine multi-scale features with inter-scale knowledge. The inter-scale relationship provides extra knowledge of tissues-of-interest in lesions for clinical examination on WSIs to improve the CD diagnosis performance. The cross-scale attention visualization represents automatic scale-awareness and distinctive contributions to disease diagnosis in MIL when learning the phenotype features at different scales in different regions, offering an external AI-based clue for multi-scale pathological image analysis.

Acknowledgements. This work is supported by Leona M. and Harry B. Helmsley Charitable Trust grant G-1903-03793, NSF CAREER 1452485, and Veterans Affairs Merit Review grants I01BX004366 and I01CX002171, and R01DK103831.

References

1. AbdulJabbar, K., et al.: Geospatial immune variability illuminates differential evolution of lung adenocarcinoma. Nat. Med. **26**(7), 1054–1062 (2020)
2. Abousamra, S., et al.: Multi-class cell detection using spatial context representation. In: Proceedings of the IEEE/CVF International Conference on Computer Vision, pp. 4005–4014 (2021)
3. Agarap, A.F.: Deep learning using rectified linear units (relu). arXiv preprint arXiv:1803.08375 (2018)
4. Bao, S., et al.: A cross-platform informatics system for the gut cell atlas: integrating clinical, anatomical and histological data. In: Medical Imaging 2021: Imaging Informatics for Healthcare, Research, and Applications, vol. 11601, pp. 8–15. SPIE (2021)
5. Bejnordi, B.E., Litjens, G., Hermsen, M., Karssemeijer, N., van der Laak, J.A.: A multi-scale superpixel classification approach to the detection of regions of interest in whole slide histopathology images. In: Medical Imaging 2015: Digital Pathology, vol. 9420, pp. 99–104. SPIE (2015)
6. Bejnordi, B.E., et al.: Diagnostic assessment of deep learning algorithms for detection of lymph node metastases in women with breast cancer. JAMA **318**(22), 2199–2210 (2017)
7. Chen, J., Cheung, H.M.C., Milot, L., Martel, A.L.: AMINN: autoencoder-based multiple instance neural network improves outcome prediction in multifocal liver metastases. In: de Bruijne, M., et al. (eds.) MICCAI 2021. LNCS, vol. 12905, pp. 752–761. Springer, Cham (2021). https://doi.org/10.1007/978-3-030-87240-3_72
8. Chen, X., He, K.: Exploring simple siamese representation learning. In: Proceedings of the IEEE/CVF Conference on Computer Vision and Pattern Recognition, pp. 15750–15758 (2021)
9. Con, D., van Langenberg, D.R., Vasudevan, A.: Deep learning vs conventional learning algorithms for clinical prediction in Crohn's disease: a proof-of-concept study. World J. Gastroenterol. **27**(38), 6476 (2021)
10. Dehaene, O., Camara, A., Moindrot, O., de Lavergne, A., Courtiol, P.: Self-supervision closes the gap between weak and strong supervision in histology. arXiv preprint arXiv:2012.03583 (2020)
11. Dimitriou, N., Arandjelović, O., Caie, P.D.: Deep learning for whole slide image analysis: an overview. Front. Med. **6**, 264 (2019)
12. Gao, R., et al.: Cancer risk estimation combining lung screening CT with clinical data elements. Radiol. Artif. Intell. **3**(6), e210032 (2021)
13. Gao, Y., et al.: Multi-scale learning based segmentation of glands in digital colorectal pathology images. In: Medical Imaging 2016: Digital Pathology, vol. 9791, pp. 175–180. SPIE (2016)
14. Gubatan, J., Levitte, S., Patel, A., Balabanis, T., Wei, M.T., Sinha, S.R.: Artificial intelligence applications in inflammatory bowel disease: emerging technologies and future directions. World J. Gastroenterol. **27**(17), 1920 (2021)
15. Hashimoto, N., et al.: Multi-scale domain-adversarial multiple-instance CNN for cancer subtype classification with unannotated histopathological images. In: Proceedings of the IEEE/CVF Conference on Computer Vision and Pattern Recognition (CVPR) (2020)

16. Hou, L., Samaras, D., Kurc, T.M., Gao, Y., Davis, J.E., Saltz, J.H.: Patch-based convolutional neural network for whole slide tissue image classification. In: Proceedings of the IEEE conference on computer vision and pattern recognition, pp. 2424–2433 (2016)
17. Ilse, M., Tomczak, J., Welling, M.: Attention-based deep multiple instance learning. In: International Conference on Machine Learning, pp. 2127–2136. PMLR (2018)
18. Kiyokawa, H., et al.: Deep learning analysis of histologic images from intestinal specimen reveals adipocyte shrinkage and mast cell infiltration to predict postoperative Crohn disease. Am. J. Pathol. **192**, 904–916 (2022)
19. Kraszewski, S., Szczurek, W., Szymczak, J., Reguła, M., Neubauer, K.: Machine learning prediction model for inflammatory bowel disease based on laboratory markers. working model in a discovery cohort study. J. Clin. Med. **10**(20), 4745 (2021)
20. Li, B., Li, Y., Eliceiri, K.W.: Dual-stream multiple instance learning network for whole slide image classification with self-supervised contrastive learning. In: Proceedings of the IEEE/CVF Conference on Computer Vision and Pattern Recognition (CVPR), pp. 14318–14328 (2021)
21. Lu, M.Y., et al.: Ai-based pathology predicts origins for cancers of unknown primary. Nature **594**(7861), 106–110 (2021)
22. Lu, M.Y., Williamson, D.F., Chen, T.Y., Chen, R.J., Barbieri, M., Mahmood, F.: Data-efficient and weakly supervised computational pathology on whole-slide images. Nat. Biomed. Eng. **5**(6), 555–570 (2021)
23. Maksoud, S., Zhao, K., Hobson, P., Jennings, A., Lovell, B.C.: Sos: selective objective switch for rapid immunofluorescence whole slide image classification. In: Proceedings of the IEEE/CVF Conference on Computer Vision and Pattern Recognition, pp. 3862–3871 (2020)
24. Mousavi, H.S., Monga, V., Rao, G., Rao, A.U.: Automated discrimination of lower and higher grade gliomas based on histopathological image analysis. J. Pathol. Inf. **6**(1), 15 (2015)
25. Schirris, Y., Gavves, E., Nederlof, I., Horlings, H.M., Teuwen, J.: Deepsmile: self-supervised heterogeneity-aware multiple instance learning for dna damage response defect classification directly from h&e whole-slide images. arXiv preprint arXiv:2107.09405 (2021)
26. Skrede, O., et al.: Deep learning for prediction of colorectal cancer outcome: a discovery and validation study. Lancet **395**(10221), 350–360 (2020)
27. Syed, S., Stidham, R.W.: Potential for standardization and automation for pathology and endoscopy in inflammatory bowel disease. Inflamm. Bowel Dis. **26**(10), 1490–1497 (2020)
28. Tokunaga, H., Teramoto, Y., Yoshizawa, A., Bise, R.: Adaptive weighting multi-field-of-view CNN for semantic segmentation in pathology. In: Proceedings of the IEEE/CVF Conference on Computer Vision and Pattern Recognition, pp. 12597–12606 (2019)
29. Wang, S., et al.: RMDL: recalibrated multi-instance deep learning for whole slide gastric image classification. Med. Image Anal. **58**, 101549 (2019)
30. Yao, H., Zhu, D., Jiang, B., Yu, P.: Negative log likelihood ratio loss for deep neural network classification. In: Arai, K., Bhatia, R., Kapoor, S. (eds.) FTC 2019. AISC, vol. 1069, pp. 276–282. Springer, Cham (2020). https://doi.org/10.1007/978-3-030-32520-6_22
31. Yao, J., Zhu, X., Jonnagaddala, J., Hawkins, N., Huang, J.: Whole slide images based cancer survival prediction using attention guided deep multiple instance learning networks. Med. Image Anal. **65**, 101789 (2020)
32. Yeshi, K., Ruscher, R., Hunter, L., Daly, N.L., Loukas, A., Wangchuk, P.: Revisiting inflammatory bowel disease: pathology, treatments, challenges and emerging therapeutics including drug leads from natural products. J. Clin. Med. **9**(5), 1273 (2020)
33. Zhu, X., Yao, J., Zhu, F., Huang, J.: Wsisa: Making survival prediction from whole slide histopathological images. In: Proceedings of the IEEE Conference on Computer Vision and Pattern Recognition, pp. 7234–7242 (2017)

Vessel Segmentation via Link Prediction of Graph Neural Networks

Hao Yu[1], Jie Zhao[2], and Li Zhang[1,3(✉)]

[1] Center for Data Science, Peking University, Beijing, China
zhangli_pku@pku.edu.cn
[2] National Engineering Laboratory for Big Data Analysis and Applications,
Peking University, Beijing, China
[3] National Biomedical Imaging Center, Peking University, Beijing, China

Abstract. The topology of the segmented vessels is essential to evaluate a vessel segmentation approach. However, most popular convolutional neural network (CNN) models, such as U-Net and its variants, pay minimal attention to the topology of vessels. This paper proposes integrating graph neural networks (GNN) and classic CNN to enhance the model performance on the vessel topology. Specifically, we first use a U-Net as our base model. Then, to form the underlying graph in GNN, we sample the corners on the skeleton of the labeled vessels as the graph nodes and use the semantic information from the base U-Net as the node features, which construct the graph edges. Furthermore, we extend the previously reported graphical connectivity constraint module (GCCM) to predict the links between different nodes to maintain the vessel topology. Experiments on DRIVE and 1092 digital subtraction angiography (DSA) images of coronary arteries dataset show that our method has achieved comparable results with the current state-of-the-art methods on classic Dice and centerline-Dice.

Keywords: Vessel segmentation · Graph neural network · Deep learning · Link prediction

1 Introduction

Retinal vessel segmentation provides essential supportive information for the clinical diagnosis of ocular diseases, such as macular degeneration, diabetic retinopathy, and glaucoma. Likewise, the anomaly changes of coronary arteries identified by the coronary segmentation may indicate hypertension, myocardial infarction, and coronary atherosclerotic disease. However, after decades of research, vessel segmentation remains challenging. One of the reasons is that the topology of vessels is exceptionally complex for classic methods to ensure the connectivity of blood vessels.

Deep learning methods based on convolutional neural networks (CNN) have achieved remarkable performance in segmentation tasks. The U-Net is proven as

X. Li et al. (Eds.): MMMI 2022, LNCS 13594, pp. 34–43, 2022.
https://doi.org/10.1007/978-3-031-18814-5_4

an effective model in medical image segmentation [11]. After that, several variants of U-Net have been proposed to improve the network architecture or training strategy to achieve better performances, such as [9,19,20]. It is worth noting that nnU-Net, an out-of-the-box tool based on U-Net, generates state-of-the-art segmentations without manual intervention in many medical segmentation tasks [4]. However, these methods are trained under evenly weighted pixel-wise losses, usually ignoring the relatively weak linkage between the vessel segments, which sabotages the topology and connectivity of the segmented vessels. To solve this problem, Mosinska et al. [10] propose a method to perform segmentation and path classification simultaneously. Hu et al. [3] propose a continuous-valued loss function based on the Betti number, which can persist homology. Notably, Shit et al. [16] introduce centerline-Dice (clDice) to encourage the segmentation model maintaining tubular structures. In this work, we also use clDice as a metric to evaluate the topology and connectivity of the vessel segmentation results.

Recently, graph neural network (GNN) has been introduced to medical image segmentation. GNN has been proved to discover the relationship between connected nodes by aggregating node features in a non-Euclidean domain, thereby improving segmentation performance. Saueressig et al. [12] construct the nodes of the graph through SLIC superpixel method [1] and transform the pixel-level segmentation of the brain tumor into the graph-level node classification. However, this method is more suitable for concentrated targets, such as lesion segmentation or natural image segmentation, other than vessels. Vessels have slender tree-like structures and complex topologies and require a more delicate design of graph construction and training. Vessel graph network (VGN), proposed by Shin et al., is the first model to embed GNN into the traditional CNN model for retinal vessel segmentation [15]. However, the overcomplex network architecture of VGN is inefficient. Li et al. [8] followed the graph construction method in VGN, and designed a graphical connectivity constraint module (GCCM) in a plug-in mode which backpropagates the information of the GNN to the CNN in training stage and significantly reduces the computational cost of the inference stage.

The above GNN-based models typically construct the graph nodes by sampling some pixels in the non-overlapping sub-regions in the image. The models then connect the nodes with edges if both nodes are on the vessels, which results in many redundant and isolated nodes. These unwanted nodes highly increase the computational cost in the graph construction and training stage. On the other hand, the aforementioned methods only use GNN as node classification, which labels the sub-regions as vessels or not. But it is not helpful to maintain the topology and connectivity of vessel segmentation results. Therefore, we consider that link prediction between nodes outweighs the mere node classification on enhancing the topology and connectivity of the segmented vessels rather than classifying graph nodes. To achieve the link prediction using GNN, Kipf et al. [6] propose two graph auto-encoders (GAE and VGAE) that reconstruct the adjacency matrix by node embeddings generated by graph convolutional network (GCN). Ahn et al. [2] improve Kipf's methods by proposing a variational graph normalized autoEncoder (VGNAE), which more effectively utilizes the node features.

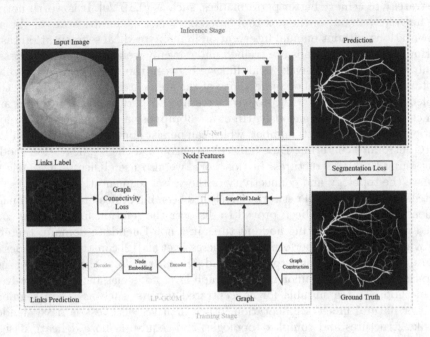

Fig. 1. The overview of our framework. The upper part is U-Net for segmentation, while the lower part is the LP-GCCM that enhances vascular connectivity. The LP-GCCM only participates in training stage but not in inference stage.

This work embeds a more topology-focused GNN into the classic CNN model to segment vessels. Inspired by Li et al. [8], we propose a novel corner-based graph construction approach and extend their original GCCM to fit the link prediction settings. The proposed graph construction approach shows more effective utilization of the semantic information from the base CNN model. It can significantly reduce the time elapsed training the GNN. Furthermore, our proposed link prediction shows an excellent ability to maintain the connectivity of the segmented vessels. On the public DRIVE dataset [17], and a private dataset of 1092 digital subtraction angiography (DSA) images of coronary arteries [22], experiments show that our method outperforms the current state-of-the-art methods. And our method produces a significantly higher result on clDice metric.

2 Methods

In this section, we describe in detail the corner-based vascular connectivity graph construction approach, the training stage of link prediction-based GCCM (LP-GCCM), and the ensemble modeling. The overview of our framework is shown in Fig. 1.

2.1   Corner-Based Vascular Connectivity Graph Construction

A graph can be described by $G = (V; E; A)$, where V is the set of nodes, E is the set of edges, and A is the adjacency matrix [21]. We divide the graph construction into five steps: node sampling, node feature generation, edge construction, adjacency matrix generation and edge label generation (shown in Fig. 2).

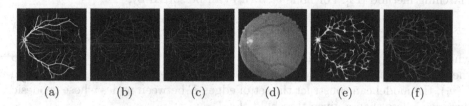

(a)   (b)   (c)   (d)   (e)   (f)

Fig. 2. Example of graph construction process. (a) Manual annotation, (b) Skeleton, (c) Corner-based node sampling (the red points represent nodes), (d) Superpixel clusters, (e) Edge construction, (f) Edge label generation (green lines represent positive edges, while blue lines represent negative edges). (Color figure online)

Node Sampling: Like in VGN and Li et al., the classic node sampling extracts pixels from fix-sized sub-regions, which is inefficient. For example, such method samples a total of 20732 nodes from the 21st image in the DRIVE dataset, however, only 3380 nodes exist edges, and about 6366 nodes are in the black background.

Therefore, we propose a corner-based graph construction method. Specifically, given a vessel manual annotation I, we apply ultimate thinning [7] to obtain the skeleton I_S of I and adopt the method in Shi et al. [14] to sample the corners on I_S as the set of graph nodes $V = \{v_i\}_{i=1}^{N_n} = \{(x_i, y_i)\}_{i=1}^{N_n}$, where N_n represents the number of corners. We set the upper limit of N_n to 1000, the Euclidean distance between the corners is greater than 5, ensuring that the corners are evenly distributed on vessels.

Node Feature Generation: Node feature generation is an important link between CNN and GNN, so we use the feature map of the last layer in CNN F, which combines multi-scale features, to generate GNN node features $f = \{f_i\}_{i=1}^{N_n}$. To increase the utilization of semantic information from F, we use the adapted SLIC [1] method to cluster each node $v_i \in V$ simultaneously. We fix the center (x_i, y_i) of v_i during processing iterations of SLIC algorithm. A cluster C_i corresponding to each v_i is created and the mean value of the features of each pixels $(cx_j, cy_j) \in C_i$ is then computed as f_i, which can be defined as,

$$f_i = \frac{\sum_{j=1}^{|C_i|} F(cx_j, cy_j)}{|C_i|}, \tag{1}$$

where $|C_i|$ represents the number of pixels in C_i. We treat f_i as the node feature of v_i, and in this work, f_i is a one-dimensional vector with 64 entries.

Edge Construction: We adopt the same edge construction method in Li et al. [8] which uses the geodesic distance as the edge construction criterion. The construction process calculates the travel time T between nodes in V by the fast marching method [13]. For node v_i, $T(v_i)$ can be solved by,

$$S \cdot |\nabla T(v_i)| = 1, \tag{2}$$

where S is the speed function, which is the ground truth (GT) of vessels, so the nodes travel faster on vessels. By calculating the travel time of each node $T(v_i)$, the model can construct the set of edges E between nodes whose geodesic distance is less than a given threshold $thre_{tt}$,

$$E = \{e_{i,j}\}_{i=1,j=1}^{N_e}, if\ T(v_i, v_j) < thre_{tt}, \tag{3}$$

where N_e represents the number of edges, and $e_{i,j}$ represents the directed edge from v_i to v_j.

Adjacency Matrix Generation: The adjacency matrix A reflects the attributes of the edges in the graph. We apply the cosine similarity between two node features to generate the adjacency matrix as follows,

$$A_{i,j} = \begin{cases} \frac{cos(f_i, f_j)}{\sum_{k \in Ner(v_i)} cos(f_i, f_k)} & e_{i,j} \in E; \\ 0 & e_{i,j} \notin E, \end{cases} \tag{4}$$

where $Ner(v_i)$ is the set of neighboring nodes of v_i.

Edge Label Generation: To provide edge labels for the link prediction, we determine whether edges are positive or negative by the distance between I_S and E. Given an edge $e_{i,j} \in E$, we can represent it with an image-level line. Our model then calculates the minimum distance of $e_{i,j}$ from I_S, and determines the distance less than the threshold $thre_{dis}$ as positive, and the others as negative. As shown in column (f) of Fig. 2, the positive edges almost coincide with I_S.

2.2   Graphical Connectivity Constraint Module

Based on the graph $G = (V; E; A)$ and node features f, we propose a LP-GCCM for enhancing vessel connectivity. GNNs can encode f through graph convolution to obtain node embeddings Z and use inner-product to decode the embeddings to reconstruct the adjacency matrix $\hat{A}$ [6],

$$\hat{A} = \sigma(Z \cdot Z^T),\ with\ Z = Encoder(f, A), \tag{5}$$

where *Encoder* is any graph convolution layers and σ is the sigmoid function. In VGNAE [2], the *Encoder* is graph normalized convolutional network (GNGN) using L2-normalization.

Following Li et al. [8], we use the plug-in mode to integrate GNN into CNN, which makes GNN constrain the vessel connectivity only during the training stage. Unlike ordinary link prediction tasks that take all existing edges as positive edges, we selectively generate edge labels, as reported in Sect. 2.1.

2.3   Network Training

Dice loss and Cross-entropy (CE) loss are widely used in medical image segmentation. We combine the two as the segmentation loss L_{Seg} to train U-net:

$$
L_{Seg} = 1 - \frac{2\sum_{i=1}^{N_p} p_i \cdot y_i + \epsilon}{\sum_{i=1}^{N_p} p_i + \sum_{i=1}^{N_p} y_i + \epsilon} - \frac{1}{N_p}\sum_{i=1}^{N_p}(y_i \cdot \log(p_i) + (1-y_i)\cdot \log(1-p_i)), \quad (6)
$$

where N_p is the number of pixels, p_i and y_i mean the probability and GT of pixel i, respectively, and ϵ is the smoothness term which is set to 1e–6.

For the LP-GCCM, we also use CE with sigmoid layer as the graph constraint connectivity loss L_{GCC},

$$
L_{GCC} = -\frac{1}{N_e}\sum_{i=1}^{N_e}(y_i \cdot \log \sigma(p_i) + (1 - y_i) \cdot \log \sigma(1 - p_i)), \quad (7)
$$

where p_i and y_i mean the probability output and the label generated in Sect. 2.1 of edge i, respectively. The loss for the whole network $L_{sum} = L_{Seg} + L_{GCC}$.

2.4   Ensemble Modeling

Due to the possible catastrophic forgetting phenomenon, plugging in GNN may undermine the performance of the base U-Net. Therefore, we ensemble the proposed method and a pure base U-Net by taking the union of their results, which significantly improves the overall segmentation.

3   Experiments and Results

In this section, We evaluate our method on DRIVE and 1092 DSA images of coronary arteries dataset, demonstrating that our method outperforms related methods in segmentation accuracy, vessel connectivity, and time cost.

3.1   Dataset

DRIVE dataset [17] is the most common benchmark that includes 40 fundus images of size 565×584 with manual annotations. Besides, we include a dataset with 1092 coronary arteries DSA images of size 512×512 with manual annotations, of which 546 images are in the training set, 218 images are in the validation set, and the remaining 328 images form the test set.

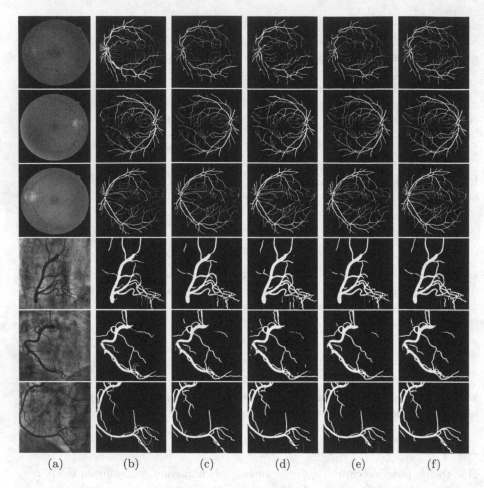

(a)   (b)   (c)   (d)   (e)   (f)

Fig. 3. Example of blood vessel segmentation results on two datasets. (a) Original images, (b) Manual annotation, (c) Baseline, (d) Li et al., (e) Our LP-GCCM only, (f) Our ensemble model. The first three rows are the results of the DRIVE, and the last three rows are the results of the coronary arteries DSA images dataset. The red boxes represent better vessel connectivity segmented by our method. (Color figure online)

3.2 Experiment Details

We use the Adam algorithm as the optimizer [5] with learning rates of 5e–4 and 5e–2 for U-Net and GCCM on both datasets. The learning rate decays by a factor of 0.85 every 20 epochs. Meanwhile, The grid interval and the weight between color similarity and spatial proximity in the SLIC method are set to 5 and 35, and the threshold $thre_{tt}$ and $thre_{dis}$ in edge and edge label construction are 25 and 1, respectively. The training epochs are 200 and 100, and the batch sizes are 2 for DRIVE and the DSA image dataset. All the experiments are implemented on NVIDIA Tesla V100 GPU.

3.3   Results

We show evaluation results by different methods in Table 1 and examples of vessel segmentation results on two datasets in Fig. 3. As the baseline of this paper, U-Net has Dice scores of 0.8149 and 0.8870 on the DRIVE and the DSA datasets. Our proposed method has Dice scores of 0.8267 and 0.8921 on two datasets, outperforming the baseline and Li's method. Furthermore, ensemble modeling can effectively improve both Dice and clDice metrics. Our method has high clDice scores of 0.8267 and 0.9206, respectively, presenting better vessel connectivity.

Table 1. Comparison on DRIVE and coronary arteries DSA images dataset

DRIVE				
Method	Accuracy	Precision	Dice	clDice
U-Net	0.9685	0.8383	0.8149	0.8147
Li et al.	0.9645	0.7773	0.8046	0.8221
Our LP-GCCM	0.9679	0.8264	0.8137	0.8210
Our ensemble model	0.9677	0.8085	**0.8176**	**0.8267**
Coronary arteries DSA images dataset				
Method	Accuracy	Precision	Dice	clDice
U-Net	0.9694	0.8392	0.8870	0.9162
Li et al.	0.9631	0.7987	0.8677	0.9073
Our LP-GCCM	0.9699	0.8458	0.8875	0.9200
Our ensemble model	0.9713	0.8521	**0.8921**	**0.9206**

4   Ablation Study

In this section, we evaluate different graph construction methods, and different downstream tasks using the same GNN model [18] on the DRIVE dataset. The results in Table 2 show that our graph construction method is more effective, and the link prediction has achieved the best performance in vessel connectivity.

Table 2. Ablation study results on graph construction method and LP-GCCM. NC and LP represent for node classification and link prediction tasks. The size of sub-region is 4 × 4 in Li's method.

Method	Task	Dice	clDice	N_n	N_e	Training time(s)	Graph constuction time(s)
Li et al.	NC	0.8046	0.8221	20732	31391.6	1312	321.0
	LP	0.8108	0.8176			1308	
Ours	NC	0.8129	0.8196	**957.4**	**7451.5**	81	**26.8**
	LP	**0.8144**	**0.8231**			70	

5   Conclusion

This paper proposes a corner-based graph construction method and a GCCM-based link prediction to maintain vessel connectivity and improve vessel segmentation performance. Despite the promising results, our method requires further investigation: 1. adaptive thresholds could be introduced to void possible disconnection of the links according to the curvature of the vessels. 2. prior knowledge in the retinal and coronary vessels may help foster the convergence of the GNNs; 3. we can further design training strategies to reduce the catastrophic forgetting issue instead of ensemble modeling. In summary, the proposed vessel segmentation can maintain vessel connectivity and topology and has the potential to provide more accurate support for the quantitatively clinical diagnosis.

Acknowledgements. This work is supported by the Grants under Beijing Natural Science Foundation (Z180001), The National Natural Science Foundation of China (NSFC) under Grants 81801778, 12090022, and 11831002.

References

1. Achanta, R., Shaji, A., Smith, K., Lucchi, A., Fua, P., Süsstrunk, S.: Slic superpixels compared to state-of-the-art superpixel methods. IEEE Trans. Pattern Anal. Mach. Intell. **34**(11), 2274–2282 (2012)
2. Ahn, S.J., Kim, M.: Variational graph normalized autoencoders. In: Proceedings of the 30th ACM International Conference on Information & Knowledge Management, pp. 2827–2831 (2021)
3. Hu, X., Li, F., Samaras, D., Chen, C.: Topology-preserving deep image segmentation. In: Advances in Neural Information Processing Systems, vol. 32 (2019)
4. Isensee, F., Jaeger, P.F., Kohl, S.A., Petersen, J., Maier-Hein, K.H.: nnu-net: a self-configuring method for deep learning-based biomedical image segmentation. Nat. Methods **18**(2), 203–211 (2021)
5. Kingma, D.P., Ba, J.: Adam: a method for stochastic optimization. arXiv preprint. arXiv:1412.6980 (2014)
6. Kipf, T.N., Welling, M.: Variational graph auto-encoders. arXiv preprint. arXiv:1611.07308 (2016)
7. Lam, L., Lee, S.W., Suen, C.Y.: Thinning methodologies-a comprehensive survey. IEEE Trans. Pattern Anal. Mach. Intell. **14**(09), 869–885 (1992)
8. Li, R., et al.: 3d graph-connectivity constrained network for hepatic vessel segmentation. IEEE J. Biomed. Health Inform. **26**(3), 1251–1262 (2021)
9. Livne, M., et al.: A U-Net deep learning framework for high performance vessel segmentation in patients with cerebrovascular disease. Front. Neurosci. **13**, 97 (2019)
10. Mosinska, A., Koziński, M., Fua, P.: Joint segmentation and path classification of curvilinear structures. IEEE Trans. Pattern Anal. Mach. Intell. **42**(6), 1515–1521 (2019)
11. Ronneberger, O., Fischer, P., Brox, T.: U-Net: convolutional networks for biomedical image segmentation. In: Navab, N., Hornegger, J., Wells, W.M., Frangi, A.F. (eds.) MICCAI 2015. LNCS, vol. 9351, pp. 234–241. Springer, Cham (2015). https://doi.org/10.1007/978-3-319-24574-4_28

12. Saueressig, C., Berkley, A., Munbodh, R., Singh, R.: A joint graph and image convolution network for automatic brain tumor segmentation. arXiv preprint. arXiv:2109.05580 (2021)
13. Sethian, J.A.: Fast marching methods. SIAM Rev. **41**(2), 199–235 (1999)
14. Shi, J., et al.: Good features to track. In: 1994 Proceedings of IEEE Conference on Computer Vision and Pattern Recognition, pp. 593–600. IEEE (1994)
15. Shin, S.Y., Lee, S., Yun, I.D., Lee, K.M.: Deep vessel segmentation by learning graphical connectivity. Med. Image Anal. **58**, 101556 (2019)
16. Shit, S., et al.: clDice-a novel topology-preserving loss function for tubular structure segmentation. In: Proceedings of the IEEE/CVF Conference on Computer Vision and Pattern Recognition, pp. 16560–16569 (2021)
17. Staal, J., Abràmoff, M.D., Niemeijer, M., Viergever, M.A., Van Ginneken, B.: Ridge-based vessel segmentation in color images of the retina. IEEE Trans. Med. Imaging **23**(4), 501–509 (2004)
18. Veličković, P., Cucurull, G., Casanova, A., Romero, A., Lio, P., Bengio, Y.: Graph attention networks. arXiv preprint. arXiv:1710.10903 (2017)
19. Wang, B., Qiu, S., He, H.: Dual encoding U-Net for retinal vessel segmentation. In: Shen, D., et al. (eds.) MICCAI 2019. LNCS, vol. 11764, pp. 84–92. Springer, Cham (2019). https://doi.org/10.1007/978-3-030-32239-7_10
20. Wang, C., Zhao, Z., Ren, Q., Xu, Y., Yu, Y.: Dense U-net based on patch-based learning for retinal vessel segmentation. Entropy **21**(2), 168 (2019)
21. Wu, Z., Pan, S., Chen, F., Long, G., Zhang, C., Philip, S.Y.: A comprehensive survey on graph neural networks. IEEE Trans. Neural Netw. Learn. Syst. **32**(1), 4–24 (2020)
22. Yu, F., et al.: Annotation-free cardiac vessel segmentation via knowledge transfer from retinal images. In: Shen, D., et al. (eds.) MICCAI 2019. LNCS, vol. 11765, pp. 714–722. Springer, Cham (2019). https://doi.org/10.1007/978-3-030-32245-8_79

A Bagging Strategy-Based Multi-scale Texture GLCM-CNN Model for Differentiating Malignant from Benign Lesions Using Small Pathologically Proven Dataset

Shu Zhang[1]([✉]), Jinru Wu[1], Sigang Yu[1], Ruoyang Wang[1], Enze Shi[1], Yongfeng Gao[2], and Zhengrong Liang[3]

[1] School of Computer Science, Northwestern Polytechnical University, Xi'an 710000, China
shu.zhang@nwpu.edu.cn
[2] Department of Radiology, Stony Brook University, Stony Brook, NY 11794, USA
[3] Department of Biomedical Engineering, Stony Brook University, Stony Brook, NY 11794, USA

Abstract. The application of deep learning (DL) methodology in the differentiation of benign and malignant lesions has drawn wide attention. However, it is extremely hard to acquire medical images with biopsy labeling, which leads to the scarcity of datasets. This is contrary to the requirement that DL algorithms need large datasets for training. To effectively learn features from small tumor datasets, a Bagging Strategy-based Multi-scale gray-level co-occurrence matrix (GLCM)-Convolutional Neural Network (BSM-GLCM-CNN) is proposed to boost the classification performance. Specifically, instead of feeding the raw image to the CNN, GLCM is used as the input of the designed model. As a texture descriptor, GLCM has the advantages of effectively representing lesion heterogeneity and of the same size for all input samples given the gray level. This work creatively partitions the GLCM to three groups to make full use of certain scale information of each group. When fusing the multi-scale texture information, the concept of bagging strategy in ensemble learning is used to improve the classification performance, where multiple base Learners are generated. Final classification results are obtained by integrating the multi-scale base Learners with the voting mechanism. Experimental results show that the proposed BSM-GLCM-CNN can successfully distinguish colonic polyps in a small dataset. The proposed method achieves an improvement from 68.00% Area Under Curve (AUC) to 90.88% AUC over other state-of-the-art models. The experimental results demonstrate the great potential of the proposed method when challenged by small pathological datasets in the medical imaging field.

Keywords: Deep learning · Bagging strategy · Multi-scale · Gray-level co-occurrence matrix · Polyp classification

X. Li et al. (Eds.): MMMI 2022, LNCS 13594, pp. 44–53, 2022.
https://doi.org/10.1007/978-3-031-18814-5_5

1 Introduction

DL has been widely evolved in recent years [1]. DL is a multi-layer network composed of a large number of neurons [2]. Given a large amount of training data, these neurons can automatically discover distinguishing features and make decisions [3]. A widely used way to distinguish features is based on the convolutional neural networks (CNN) in the DL architecture [4]. CNN has been successfully applied to the task of classification of natural images, such as face recognition [5]. There are also many reports of successful CNN application in the task of diagnosis of various diseases [6], e.g. the application of CNN for early differentiation or diagnosis of lung nodules before their malignant transformation into lung cancer [7, 8].

However, in these diagnosis studies, the CNN models focused more on learning from the raw computed tomography (CT) images [9, 10]. One difficulty is that limited features learned from lesions of uncertain size and morphology in the raw images [11]. To consider this uncertainty of the raw images, a large number of studies have preprocessed the raw images before training the models [12, 13]. For instance, Ma et al. segmented the raw images, performed the first- and second-order derivatives for geometric analysis [12]. And then linear discriminate analysis (LDA) was applied to extract deep features from the raw image data, where the LDA was adopted to reduce the dimensionality of the feature [13]. The other difficulty is that datasets are usually scarce in medical imaging-based diagnosis, particularly for cancer imaging. Utilizing small datasets to train the deep learning models usually results in suboptimal classification. Some studies sought to expand the dataset volume to tackle this problem at its source, such as, data warping and synthetic over-sampling were investigated to create additional training samples [14]. When facing the difficulty of small dataset classification, ensemble learning can be another choice. Ensemble learning has advantages in dealing with scarce datasets and is efficient in classification tasks by building and combining multiple DL algorithms [15], which could reduce differences of automated decision systems and improve classification accuracy [16]. For instance, a multi-view ensemble learning-based voting mechanism was presented to boost the classification performance in small datasets [17]. Alternatively, the small datasets can be divided into multiple subsets to train the model to form an adaptive system based on ensemble learning [18].

Despite the great effort of mitigating the uncertainty of the raw images and the scarcity of datasets, the difficulty of obtaining satisfactory differentiation malignant from benign lesions remains. According to above-mentioned issues, we summarize the factors restricting the improvement of polyp classification into two categories. One is related to the variations of polyp shape and size due to pathological changes as represented in the raw images, so it is hard for DL models to extract, summarize and further learn effective features. The other is the small data volume because of the difficulty of collecting large data volume with pathological ground truth from the patients. Hence, how to use small image data volume for classification task of tumor polyps is still a formidable challenge.

To address the limitations mentioned above, a BSM-GLCM-CNN model is proposed in this work. This paper uses CT data of colonic polyps as study material to validate our method. The innovation of the model can be summarized into two folds. First, to address the uncertainty of CT raw images of the polyps, this study uses GLCM instead of the raw CT images as the input of CNN models and divides GLCM into three groups to allow the model to learn certain scale information. As a method of describing and analyzing texture features, GLCM has excellent properties such as size consistency, shape and scaling invariance [19]. So GLCM-based CNN does not need the adjustment of CT raw image sizes and preserve the uniformity of feature extraction from the raw images. Second, to address the accuracy of the model is hard to improve due to the scarcity of CT raw images, this study adopts the bagging strategy [20], where a parallel ensemble learning can be generated simultaneously. Specifically, this study randomly generates multiple groups of Random Train Test sets (RTTsets) to train base Learners on multi-scale GLCM texture features, i.e. letting all Learners vote and finally integrate the voting results through specific combination tactics. It greatly reduces generalization error and alleviates the problems caused by small datasets. The BSM-GLCM-CNN model improves the accuracy of performing the polyp classification compared with several existing state-of-the-art classification methods.

2   Methods

2.1   Dataset and Preprocessing

59 patients are provided with 63 polyps containing 31 benign and 32 malignant polyps. Benign polyps include four categories, i.e., Serrated Adenoma (3 cases), Tubular Adenoma (2 cases), Tubulovillous Adenoma (21 cases), Villous Adenoma (5 cases). The malignant is Adenocarcinoma only (32 cases). The polyp size ranges from 3 to 8 cm (an average of 4.2 cm). A routine clinical non-contrast CT scanning protocol covering the entire abdomen scanned the patients. More than 400 image slices are obtained for each CT image, every slice size is setting to 512×512, and every image voxel is nearly cubic with 1mm. Experts adopted a semi-automated segmentation algorithm to draw contour of polyp image slice inside the CT abdominal image volume.

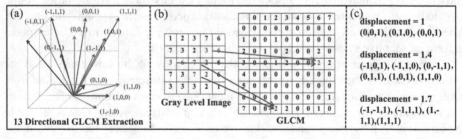

Fig. 1. The illustration of (a) the GLCM in 13 directions. (b) the process of GLCM formation. (c) the multi-scale displacement.

GLCM is a method to extract statistical texture features from raw images [21]. The co-occurrence matrix (CM) describes the displacement and direction relationship between pixel pairs in the digital image, the definition is as follows:

$$C_{i,j}(d, \theta) = \sum_{p \in V} \begin{cases} 1 & \text{if } I(p + d(\cos\theta, \sin\theta)) = j \\ 0 & \text{otherwise} \end{cases} \quad (1)$$

where I is the gray value of the raw CT image, p is a point inside the plane where the image is located, and $I_{(p)}$ is pixel value located at point p, i and j represent a group of pixels inside the image, and d is the distance from point p to other point in the direction of θ. As shown in Fig. 1(a), 13 sample directions are presented to describe the entire object [19]. Figure 1(b) shows examples of how to generate GLCM from raw grayscale images. In this work, by using the concept of multi-scale, the corresponding generated GLCM of 13 directions are divided into three scales because of the different displacement size, where the illustration is shown in Fig. 1(c), and the number of GLCM of each scale are 3, 6 and 4 respectively. It is hypothesized that the multi-scale wise grouping can improve the classification performance comparing treating 13 directions as a whole group. The grayscale value is fixed at 32.

2.2 The Structure of Bagging Strategy-Based Multi-scale GLCM-CNN

An overview of the proposed framework is presented in Fig. 2(a). The GLCM divided Data1, Data and Data3 according to the different scales are the input of the model, and the distribution of data is shown in Fig. 2(b). The details of CNN Learners for each scale are shown in Fig. 2(c), which is the same with the scale Learner mentioned in Fig. 2(a). In Fig. 2(a), bagging strategy [20] is a famous representative of a parallel ensemble learning algorithm, it is adopted in this model to study the common information from RTTsets; Multi-scale GLCM-CNN is designed to study each RTTset.

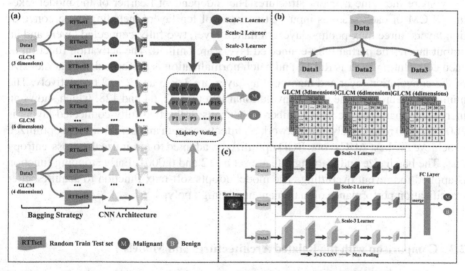

Fig. 2. An overview of (a) the BSM-GLCM-CNN framework. (b) the distribution of data. (c) the training process and concrete structure of GLCM-CNN.

Bagging Strategy. In this model, the data of each scale is divided into the training sets and testing sets randomly to generate RTTset, as shown in Fig. 2(a). 15 RTTsets are generated for each scale. For each RTTset, 31 samples (16 positive samples and

15 negative samples) are randomly selected as the test set, the training set contains the remaining 32 samples (16 positive samples and 16 negative samples). The RTTsets of different scales are used to train the models Scale-1 Learner, Scale-2 Learner and Scale-3 Learner respectively. We trained 15 base Learner for each scale. And each Learner generates a classification result. Then, all results of base Learners will be combined by a classical method of ensemble learning, the majority voting mechanism, to generate the final prediction of polyp classification. This work combines the more effective texture information learned by different Learners and RTTsets to obtain an excellent final classification effect. The majority voting mechanism can be described as follows:

$$
H(x) = \begin{cases} c_j \ if \ \sum_{i=1}^{T} h_i^j(x) > \frac{1}{2} \sum_{k=1}^{N} \sum_{i=1}^{T} h_i^k(x) \\ reject \qquad\qquad\qquad otherwise \end{cases}
\tag{2}
$$

where h represents a Learner, T means there are T Learners, and N means there are N categories. When the classification result of category j by T Learners is more than half of the total votes, category j is predicted; otherwise, the classification is rejected.

Multi-scale GLCM-CNN. The detailed CNN model architecture is shown in Fig. 2(c) using 13 directional GLCM. According to different scales of inputs, three CNN architectures are defined as Scale-1 Learner, Scale-2 Learner and Scale-3 Learner. It also corresponds to the blue circle, green square and pink triangle severally in Fig. 2(a). They share the same network structure. The independent Learner of the model takes the GLCM of each scale as inputs. It consists of ten layers including three convolution layers, three max-pooling layers, a flatten layer, two fully-connected layers and an output layer. The partial fully-connected layers are omitted. The activation function of each convolution layer is ReLU, and batch normalization is performed. The kernel size of the convolution layer and max-pooling layer are 3×3 and 2×2 respectively. The number of neurons in the three convolutional layers is 32, 64 and 128, which shows an increasing characteristic. The number of neurons in the two fully-connected layers is 1000 and 100 respectively. The network architecture depth and kernel size are optimized to achieve the best AUC score. SGD optimizer is adopted to minimize the cross-entropy loss. The batch size and learning rate are set as 12 and 0.0001. Early stopping function is applied to prevent overfitting. The model adopts soft-max function to acquire better classification performance of malignant and benign polyps.

2.3   Comparison with the Related Architectures and Models

To explore an effective approach using this small dataset to differentiate benign and malignant polyps, this study proposes a bunch of comparison architectures/models to present the classification performances. To pursue the best GLCM-CNN-based models, we proposed three other architectures, they are Single-scale, One-channel and Three-scale GLCM-CNN. At the same time, we proposed two models based on bagging strategy to chase for the better classification effects, namely Bagging Strategy-based Single-scale and One-channel GLCM-CNN.

Three-Scale, Single-Scale and One-Channel GLCM-CNN. Details of the structures are proposed here. Three-scale GLCM-CNN architecture is shown in Fig. 2(c). The GLCM of three scales are designed as the inputs and the Three-scale GLCM-CNN structure consists of three parallel scale Learners. After the parallel training of Scale-1 Learner, Scale-2 Learner and Scale-3 Learner, the outputs of three Learners are merged using concatenate function, which takes the nonuniformity of sampling direction into consideration, and two fully connected layers are adopted to achieve the classification.

Single-scale GLCM-CNN is presented to study whether information of single scale has the greatest influence on the final classification effect. The network structure is that Scale-1, Scale-2 and Scale-3 Learner learn independently using Data1, Data2 and Data3 without affecting each other.

One-channel GLCM-CNN is proposed for training all 13 directional GLCM without adopting the concept of scales. GLCM in 13 directions as a whole is inputted to one channel for training, and the model structure and specific parameters are the same as Single-scale GLCM-CNN.

Bagging Strategy-Based Single-Scale and One-Channel GLCM-CNN. Bagging Strategy-based Single-scale and One-channel GLCM-CNN both use the same CNN model and algorithm, the only difference is the data input. The former model uses GLCM of each single scale, and the latter one adopts 13 directional GLCM to be fed into one channel for training. Specifically, for each Random Train Validation Test set (RTVTsets), 31 samples are selected as the test set randomly, validation set and training set are further separated from the remaining 32 samples in the rest of amount. And the training set and the validation set are empirically settled as 24:8, which relatively outperforms other ratios. Similar to the RTTsets, RTVTsets will also be randomly generated 15 times. The RTVTset was utilized to train the models by Scale-1 Learner, Scale-2 Learner and Scale-3 Learner, so 15 Scale-1, 15 Scale-2, and 15 Scale-3 Learners are performed respectively. These Learners were sorted by the performance and upward trend of validation accuracy (val_acc), and about 10 Learners with excellent classification results are screened out among the 15 Learners. The predicted accuracies of each scale are combined with soft voting of ensemble learning to generate the final classification respectively. In addition, we also trained 15 One-channel GLCM-CNNs, and they are also combined with the soft voting mechanism.

The a represents a sample, $i (= 1, 2, 3 \dots 15)$ defines as a base Learner. The predictive value for sample a is $P_i(a)$ ($0 < P_i(a) < 1$), the set of Learners as I, then take the subset of I as J, and on this subset, the soft voting predictive value of sample is:

$$P_J(a) = \sum_{i \in J} \frac{P_i(a)}{card(J)} \tag{3}$$

where $card(J)$ represents the number of elements in set J, that is the number of trained base Learners, and $P_J(a)$ is the predictive probability of the test set after the combination of the selected base Learners.

2.4 Comparison with Existing Methods

The study uses GLCM as the feature to classify polyps, alleviating the need of the raw image size being not fixed and improving the polyp classification performance. To verify this idea, a comparison experiment is introduced [11], R-IMG, C-IMG and M-IMG are three models to classify the polyps by using raw CT images [11]. Specifically, R-IMG was to randomly select an image slice each polyp. Another method was to take the largest area slice as input, called C-IMG. Multi-channel CNN architecture was used to treat each image slice as a separate channel input that learned combined features from multiple slices, called M-IMG.

3 Results

3.1 Classification Performance of Proposed BSM-GLCM-CNN

To investigate the effectiveness of multi-scale architecture and bagging strategy on classification performance, an experiment of BSM-GLCM-CNN was carried out. Here, ten individual experiments were performed using randomly generated RTTsets every time. Based on Table 1, we achieved relatively robust classification performance, the best AUC of classification performance is achieved as high as 96.67%, the ACC, SEN and SPE reach 96.77%, 100.00% and 86.77% respectively.

Table 1. The classification results of BSM-GLCM-CNN model.

Experiment	AUC	ACC	SEN	SPE	Experiment	AUC	ACC	SEN	SPE
1	87.08	87.10	87.50	86.77	6	90.21	90.32	93.75	86.67
2	90.21	90.32	93.75	86.77	7	93.54	93.55	93.75	93.33
3	93.33	93.55	100.00	86.77	8	93.54	93.55	100.00	86.77
4	96.77	96.77	100.00	93.33	9	90.21	90.32	93.75	86.77
5	90.42	90.32	87.50	93.33	10	83.54	83.87	93.33	73.33

3.2 Effectiveness of Related Architectures and Models

To compare the effectiveness between the proposed method and other architectures/models, this study also provided the Single-scale, One-channel and Three-scale GLCM-CNN and Bagging Strategy-based Single-scale and One-channel GLCM-CNN method to conduct an experiment on polyp classification. The experiment results of these scenarios are presented in Table 2. Among the GLCM-CNNs, it can be clearly observed that the Three-scale GLCM-CNN has the highest AUC (81.62%) and the best classification effect for malignant and benign polyps, the AUC of 13 directional GLCM-based One-channel CNN model is the second place, the AUC reaches 79.25%. Among the three Single-scale Learners, Scale-1 Learner has the best overall polyp classification performance with an AUC of 77.36%, while the identification performance of Scale-2 and Scale-3 Learner is slightly worse.

The results indicate two primary points. First, it can be seen that the classification performance of Three-scale GLCM-CNN is superior to other GLCM-CNNs. Second,

Table 2. The classification results of the different methods.

Methods		AUC	ACC	SEN	SPE
GLCM-CNN	Scale_1 Learner	77.36 ± 6.42	77.42 ± 6.57	71.67 ± 13.34	83.56 ± 18.15
	Scale_2 Learner	73.85 ± 8.68	73.55 ± 9.38	64.58 ± 23.35	83.11 ± 10.35
	Scale_3 Learner	73.88 ± 8.16	73.55 ± 8.72	63.75 ± 23.76	84.00 ± 17.05
	One-channel	79.25 ±6. 47	79.14 ± 6.65	75.83 ± 15.46	82.67 ± 10.27
	Three-scale	81.62 ± 6.50	81.29 ± 6.81	76.25 ± 12.54	86.67 ±7. 13
Bagging Strategy-based GLCM-CNN	Scale_1 Learner	84.17 ± 3.10	84.20 ± 3.04	85.00 ± 6.96	83.33 ± 8.56
	Scale_2 Learner	80.82 ± 2.60	80.97 ± 2.68	83.75 ± 9.76	76.00 ± 9.98
	Scale_3 Learner	80.98 ± 2.67	80.97 ± 2.68	80.63 ± 12.01	81.33 ± 12.22
	One-channel	82.58 ± 3.87	82.50 ± 3.90	85.00 ± 10.15	80.00 ± 11.16
	Proposed multi-scale	**90.88 ± 3.51**	**90.97 ± 3.47**	**94.33 ± 4.38**	**87.33 ± 5.54**

among the three Single-scale CNNs, the classification performance of Scale-1 Learner is better than the other two Learners. In the case that the network structure of three Single-scale Learners is the same, such results elucidate that GLCM in the direction of displacement equals 1 (in Fig. 1(c)) is more suitable to classify the polyps, compared with Scale-2 and Scale-3, and Scale-1should contain much more valuable features.

The proposed Bagging Strategy-based GLCM-CNN polyp classification performance is shown in Table 2. Scale-1 Learner based on bagging strategy prominently improved the AUC from 77.36% of Scale-1 Learner to an average of 84.17%. The standard deviation narrows from 6.42% to 3.10%. Both Scale-2 Learner and Scale-3 Learner have varying degrees of enhancement. Meanwhile, the AUC of One-channel GLCM-CNN increased from 79.25% to 82.58%. Compared with Three-scale GLCM-CNN, the proposed BSM-GLCM-CNN increases from 81.62% to 90.88%. These results successfully demonstrated the effectiveness of the proposed bagging strategy.

According to the advantages of the bagging strategy, the classification error caused by the instability of a single base Learner is reduced, thus the classification performance is dramatically improved. It supports our ideas that bagging strategy in ensemble learning can benefit the polyp classification on limited medical datasets. Comparing the classification performance of the above models, the best classification performance is observed by BSM-GLCM-CNN model, it proves that classifiers combining all three scale Learners have superiority than single scale Learner, which confirms our initial hypothesis that different texture information integration can further improve the classification effect.

Overall, our results successfully demonstrate the superiority of BSM-GLCM-CNN when pathologically proven data sets are minuscule.

3.3 Comparison Experiments with Existing Methods

To compare the classification performance between raw images and GLCM images, the performances of different methods are compared and summarized in Table 3, the AUC of the proposed BSM-GLCM-CNN is much higher than raw CT-CNN methods. Around 20% improvement is obtained, which shows the super preponderance of using texture features as the input of CNN models when dealing with polyp CT images.

Table 3. The comparison between the proposed BSM-GLCM-CNN and other methods.

Methods		AUC	ACC	SEN	SPE
Raw CT Image-based CNN	R-IMG	60.00	60.00	66.00	54.00
	C-IMG	67.00	64.00	69.00	59.00
	M-IMG	68.00	74.00	76.00	50.00
BSM-GLCM-CNN		**90.88**	**90.97**	**94.33**	**87.33**

Overall, our results consistently prove that proposed BSM-GLCM-CNN achieves the best classification performance. It shows the huge benefits obtained both from GLCM texture features and bagging strategy, which reveals the great power to deal with the small pathologically proven medical image dataset.

4   Conclusion

In this paper, we proposed a BSM-GLCM-CNN model to improve the performance of classifying benign and malignant colonic polyps from pathologically proven small sample size. In this method, 15 base Learners of three scales are trained respectively, and the classification results of these 45 base Learners are voted to obtain the final lifting effect. The advantage of feature learning ability of different base Learners is reflected by the bagging mechanism and voting mechanism. And the experimental results demonstrate that our proposed method has great potential when dealing with small sample sizes. Not only the problem of low accuracy and poor effectiveness of the method brought by small sample sizes is solved, but also the problem of poor robustness of the method brought by small sample sizes is mitigated.

References

1. Yan, Z.: Multi-instance multi-stage deep learning for medical image recognition. In: Deep Learning for Medical Image Analysis, pp. 83–104 (2017)
2. Eddy, D.: Screening for colorectal cancer. Ann. Intern. Med. **113**, 373–384 (1990)

3. Hao, X., Zhang, G., Ma, S.: Deep Learning. Int. J. Semant. Comput. **10**(03), 417–439 (2016)
4. Sun, X., Wu, P., Hoi, S.: Face Detection using deep learning: an improved faster RCNN approach. Neurocomputing **299**(JUL.19), 42–50 (2018)
5. Qin, H., Yan, J., Xiu, L., et al.: Joint training of cascaded CNN for face detection. In: 2016 IEEE Conference on Computer Vision and Pattern Recognition (CVPR). IEEE (2016)
6. Shen, D., Wu, G., Suk, H.I.: Deep learning in medical image analysis. Annu. Rev. Biomed. Eng. **19**(1), 221–248 (2017)
7. Wang, H., Zhao, T., Li, L.C., et al.: A hybrid CNN feature model for pulmonary nodule malignancy risk differentiation. J. Xray Sci. Technol. **26**(2), 1–17 (2018)
8. Tan, J., Huo, Y., et al.: Expert knowledge-infused deep learning for automatic lung nodule detection. J. X-Ray Sci. Technol. **27**, 17–35 (2018)
9. Pawełczyk, K., et al.: Towards detecting high-uptake lesions from lung CT scans using deep learning. In: Battiato, S., Gallo, G., Schettini, R., Stanco, F. (eds.) ICIAP 2017. LNCS, vol. 10485, pp. 310–320. Springer, Cham (2017). https://doi.org/10.1007/978-3-319-68548-9_29
10. Liu, X., Hou, F., Qin, H., et al.: Multi-view multi-scale CNNs for lung nodule type classification from CT images. Pattern Recognit. (2018). S0031320317305186
11. Tan, J., Pickhardt, P.J., Gao, Y., et al.: 3D-GLCM CNN: a 3-dimensional gray-level co-occurrence matrix based CNN model for polyp classification via CT colonography. IEEE Trans. Med. Imaging **PP**(99), 1 (2019)
12. Ming, M., Wang, H., Song, B., et al.: Random forest based computer-aided detection of polyps in CT colonography. In: 2014 IEEE Nuclear Science Symposium and Medical Imaging Conference (NSS/MIC). IEEE (2016)
13. Lakshmanaprabu, S.K., Mohanty, S.N., Shankar, K., et al.: Optimal deep learning model for classification of lung cancer on CT images. Future Gener. Comput. Syst. **92**(MAR.), 374–382 (2019)
14. Wong, S.C., Gatt, A., Stamatescu, V., et al.: Understanding data augmentation for classification: when to warp. IEEE (2016)
15. Qi, Y.: Ensemble Machine Learning. Springer, USA (2012)
16. Polikar, R.: Ensemble learning. Scholarpedia
17. Chen, Y., Li, D., Zhang, X., et al.: Computer aided diagnosis of thyroid nodules based on the devised small-datasets multi-view ensemble learning. Med. Image Anal. **67**(1), 101819 (2021)
18. Fan, C., Hou, B., Zheng, J., et al.: A surrogate-assisted particle swarm optimization using ensemble learning for expensive problems with small sample datasets. Appl. Soft Comput. **91**, 106242 (2020)
19. Hu, Y., Liang, Z., Song, B., et al.: Texture feature extraction and analysis for polyp differentiation via computed tomography colonography. IEEE Trans. Med. Imaging **35**(6), 1522–1531 (2016)
20. Breiman, L.: Bagging predictors. Mach. Learn. **24**, 123–140 (1996)
21. Hua, B.O., Fu-Long, M.A., Jiao, L.C.: Research on computation of GLCM of image texture. Acta Electron. Sin. **1**(1), 155–158 (2006)

Liver Segmentation Quality Control in Multi-sequence MR Studies

Yi-Qing Wang[✉] and Giovanni Palma

IBM Watson Health Imaging, Rue Alfred Kastler, 91400 Orsay, France
{yi-qing.wang,giovanni.palma}@ibm.com

Abstract. For an automated liver disease diagnosis system, the ability to assess the liver segmentation quality in the absence of ground truth is crucial. Because it helps detect algorithm failures at inference time so that erroneous outputs can be prevented from impacting the diagnosis accuracy. In addition, it can be used to quality check annotated data for training and testing purposes. In this paper, we introduce the concept of liver profile as the basis for an exploratory data analysis approach to identifying poorly segmented images in multi-sequence MR liver studies.

1 Introduction

Liver segmentation is key to automated liver disease diagnosis [7]. The ability to assess the segmentation quality in the absence of ground truth is thus of interest. It allows to detect algorithm failures at inference time, which is critically important in practice because an erroneous liver segmentation may lead to errors in downstream tasks such as lesion detection [3,4,12,17,18] and image registration [1,9], thereby negatively impacting the overall diagnosis accuracy. Additionally, this ability can also help ensure the quality of annotated training and test datasets by identifying poor (image, segmentation mask) pairs, potentially resulting in better algorithms and more accurate performance evaluation.

The quality of liver segmentation, either by human annotators or by an algorithm, depends on the quality of the medical images under analysis. Strongly degraded images generally result in inaccurate segmentations. However, it is hard to quantify image quality in absolute terms, because images of good quality for one task can be poor for another [2]. For instance, in a medical image, it can be easy to ascertain the presence of a liver lesion. But its measurement and characterization can prove difficult if its textural details are hard to discern. For this reason, human experts tend to disagree with each other when it comes to rating medical images in terms of their overall quality [6,13,15], especially when they are trained in different medical fields [11].

How to automate segmentation quality assessment without access to ground truth has drawn some attention lately. Most existing methods are of supervised nature and need a set of well annotated samples to begin with. For example, the work [10] suggests to train a SVM-based regressor on geometric, intensity and gradient features to predict several segmentation error metrics with respect to

X. Li et al. (Eds.): MMMI 2022, LNCS 13594, pp. 54–62, 2022.
https://doi.org/10.1007/978-3-031-18814-5_6

ground truth. Similarly, a framework was presented in [16] which uses a model to evaluate an image's segmentation quality by checking its consistency with some known annotated samples. In a few recent works [5,8,14], the authors proposed to use uncertainty information from model produced probabilistic segmentation maps. Although these methods can be used to detect segmentation failures at inference time, they do not lend themselves easily to training data quality control because manual annotations are almost always binary valued.

In this work, we propose an exploratory data analysis approach to assessing liver segmentation quality in MR studies of the abdomen. It is based on the following observations: 1) an MR study typically consists of multi-sequence volumes and 2) within a study, all the volumes portray the same liver. Therefore, a study's well segmented volumes should yield consistent liver size statistics.

This paper is organized as follows. We first introduce the concept of liver profile and describe its properties. Next we propose a simple algorithm to estimate the liver profile from a multi-sequence liver study and demonstrate its effectiveness at detecting incorrectly segmented image slices. Finally we conclude and discuss future work.

2   Liver Profile

2.1   Definition

Consider a human liver. We define its *profile* as a function that maps a transverse plane to its corresponding liver cross-sectional area. By definition, it thus requires an infinity of axial liver slices and cannot be computed directly. Since the liver is a smooth three dimensional object, its profile must be continuous. Therefore, it can be estimated from a medical scan produced by imagining techniques such as CT and MR, which samples liver slices on a regular interval.

Specifically, consider an n-slice axial liver scan with slice spacing equal to s_z (in millimeters). Let S_i denote the area in square millimeters of the liver cross-section captured by the scan's i-th slice. Let ϕ be an interpolation through the points $\{(i, S_i)\}_{i=0,\dots,n-1}$. For example, the linear interpolation leads to

$$\phi(x) = (S_{\lfloor x \rfloor + 1} - S_{\lfloor x \rfloor})(x - \lfloor x \rfloor) + S_{\lfloor x \rfloor}, \ x \in [0, n-1) \qquad (1)$$

where $\lfloor x \rfloor$ denotes the largest integer less than or equal to $x \in \mathbb{R}$. The interpolation is then scaled to result in the *scan profile* $P(t) := \phi(t/s_z)$. Over its *support* $\{t | P(t) > 0\}$, the scan profile can be considered as an approximation of the liver profile. The support's length is referred to as the scan's *liver span*.

Note that in Eq. (1), it is an arbitrary choice to give the index of zero to the scan's first slice. Instead, we could set its index to another value, such as 1, and maintain the same concept of scan profile. In other words, both liver and scan profile are uniquely defined only up to a translation.

2.2 Properties

In the absence of major clinical events (such as a partial hepatectomy), a liver tends to have a rather static profile over a short period of time. Moreover, as long as a person's longitudinal axis points to the same direction, their liver axial cross-sectional areas are relatively insensitive to rigid body motions. As a result, a patient's various well performed scans should lead to similar-looking scan profiles, all of which resemble the same underlying liver profile.

Though the liver profiles may vary in shape from person to person (see Fig. 1), they have an asymmetrical bell shape in general. It is because the liver cross-sectional area usually peaks at a transverse plane which passes through both left and right liver lobes and gradually decreases as we move the plane towards the liver's superior or inferior surfaces.

2.3 Estimation

Generally speaking, a scan profile is a noisy and partial estimate of its corresponding liver profile. Its approximation quality depends on the scan's slice spacing, voxel resolution and the accuracy of liver cross-sectional area measurements. A smaller slice spacing, finer voxel resolution and more accurate liver segmentation lead to a scan profile of higher approximation quality.

For patients who have undergone multiple liver scans, it is possible to obtain an even better estimation of their liver profiles than the individual scan profiles themselves. To do so, consider a patient's m scan profiles $\{P_i\}_{i=1,...,m}$. Their supports, as defined previously, are of relative value because two different scans rarely portray the same abdominal region. However, since all the scan profiles describe the same liver, we can find a common coordinate system to represent them.

Without loss of generality, let us assume that the patient's first scan profile P_1 has the greatest liver span. We fix it as the reference and translate the other scan profiles to align with it individually. To this end, we use the following metric to assess the quality of alignment between two positive valued functions with finite support

$$\text{agreement}(f, g) = \frac{\int_{\{t \mid f(t)>0, g(t)>0\}} \min(f(t), g(t))dt}{\int_{\{t \mid f(t)>0, g(t)>0\}} \max(f(t), g(t))dt} \tag{2}$$

which is the Jaccard index of the areas underneath these two functions restricted to their common support. Aligning a scan profile thus amounts to finding its optimally translated version that has the maximum agreement with the reference.

Algorithm 1: Liver Profile Estimation

Data: m scan profiles $\{P_i\}_{i=1,\ldots,m}$
Result: m aligned scan profiles and estimated liver profile P^*
$\alpha \leftarrow 0$;
$i \leftarrow 0$;
$P_0^* \leftarrow$ the scan profile with the greatest liver span;
while $\alpha < 0.99$ *and* $i < 5$ **do**
     Align all the scan profiles with P_0^*;
     $P_1^* \leftarrow$ pointwise median of the aligned scan profiles i.e. Eq. (3);
     $\alpha \leftarrow$ agreement(P_0^*, P_1^*);
     $i \leftarrow i + 1$;
     $P_0^* \leftarrow P_1^*$;
end
$P^* \leftarrow P_0^*$;

Once all the scan profiles have been aligned, we may estimate the liver profile. Specifically, the estimator's support is defined as the union of those of the aligned scan profiles and its values are set pointwise to the median of the aligned scan profiles. It leads to

$$P^*(t) = \text{median} \cup_{1 \leq i \leq m, P_i(t) > 0} \{P_i(t)\}, \ t \in \cup_{1 \leq i \leq m} \{t | P_i(t) > 0\} \qquad (3)$$

where we continue to use P_i to denote an aligned scan profile.

Next, we substitute the estimated liver profile P^* for P_1 and align the entire set of scan profiles again with this new reference. These two operations are then repeated until successively obtained P^* stabilizes, which usually takes less than 5 iterations. We call the estimate P^* from the final iteration the patient's *estimated liver profile*. This procedure's pseudo code is provided in Algorithm 1.

3   Experiments

3.1   Data

Let us first describe our data. It is a private collection of 70 MR studies of adult patients from three different hospitals. The number of volumes per study varies from 4 to 11, totaling 558 volumes in all. They were acquired using various T1, T2 and diffusion weighted MR sequences with slice spacing ranging from 2 mm to 11 mm. A team of radiologists examined them one volume at a time and created the liver masks for the entire dataset, leading to 28458 marked slices.

Quality checking the annotated volumes one by one is tedious and cannot scale to larger datasets. We now describe how the liver profile can help us quickly identify the likely inaccurate segmentation masks. We had experimented with both linear and cubic spline interpolation schemes for constructing scan profiles. They yielded little difference. Therefore, for simplicity, we chose linear interpolation i.e. Eq. (1).

3.2   Exploratory Analysis at the Volume Level

Study-wise, the scan profiles from our annotated volumes are broadly consistent. To show it, we used the agreement metric defined in Eq. (2). Specifically, for the aligned scan profiles of a study, we are interested in their individual agreement with the study's estimated liver profile. Clearly, those who agree with the estimated liver profile agree well with themselves, too. To simplify the presentation, in the following, we call an aligned scan profile's agreement with its estimated liver profile its *coherence score*, which thus also takes values in the interval $[0, 1]$.

A typical MR study consists of volumes with varying slice spacing and voxel resolution, leading to scan profiles of different approximation quality. As a result, their coherence scores rarely equal 1. For example, the aligned scan profiles shown in Fig. 1 and Fig. 4, though they agree with their respective estimated liver profile, have coherence score ranging from 0.96 to 0.99.

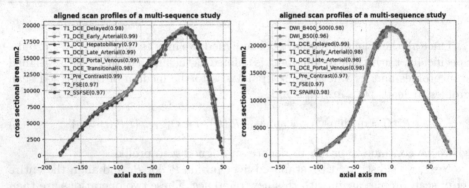

Fig. 1. Aligned scan profiles of two annotated multi-sequence MR liver studies from two different patients. They are consistent within the study. In the legend, we print for each scan profile its coherence score. These two examples show that the liver profile varies in shape across people.

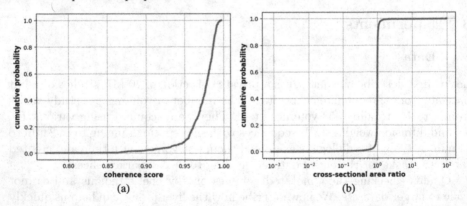

Fig. 2. (a) Plots the cumulative distribution function (CDF) of the 558 coherence scores. They are mainly distributed close to 1. In fact, 90% of them exceed 0.95. (b) Shows the CDF of the ratio between the segmented and expected liver cross-sectional area of the marked slices. The distribution of this slice-level statistic is concentrated around 1, indicating that the two area measures broadly agree.

We ran Algorithm 1 on our data one study at a time. It resulted in as many coherence scores as there are volumes in our data. Figure 2a plots their cumulative distribution function. Most of them indeed lied close to 1. Specifically, 90% of these volumes had a coherence score above 0.95. To detect inaccurate segmentations at the volume level, we thus retrieved the 55 volumes and their liver masks corresponding to the lowest 10% of the obtained coherence scores. They belonged to a total of 47 studies, each of which had at most 2 of these volumes. After a visual inspection, we found that among them, 43 annotated volumes with the lowest coherence scores were faulty because of either bad image quality or a visible segmentation error. See Fig. 3 for an example.

3.3 Exploratory Analysis at the Slice Level

For these faulty segmentations, their aligned scan profiles also help locate where the faults occur. It is because they help identify the image slices whose segmented liver cross-sectional area differs considerably from what is expected from their corresponding estimated liver profile at the same axial axis locations. In the absence of exceptional medical conditions which reduced or expanded the liver size, such a disagreement suggests a segmentation error, which may also be caused by bad image quality.

Therefore, we can use the aligned scan profiles to explore potential segmentation errors at the slice level. Specifically, for every annotated slice, we computed the ratio between its segmented liver cross-sectional area and the expected area from its corresponding estimated liver profile at the same axial axis location. It resulted in 28458 sample values whose cumulative distribution function is shown in Fig. 2b. As expected, this statistic is concentrated around 1. Too high or too low a ratio thus indicates a segmentation error (see Fig. 3).

3.4 Span Disparity

The liver profile also helps identify an additional subset of annotated volumes, which exhibit *span disparity*. It occurs when the liver is only partially observed in the image volume. This can originate from two possible causes. First, the scan's axial range is insufficient to cover the whole liver, leading to a *partial acquisition*. Second, part of the scanned liver fails to be recognized due to measurement errors or poor image quality. This latter results in a *partial segmentation*. Regardless of the cause, our approach allows to estimate such a volume's missing liver portions in a straightforward manner. See Fig. 4a for an illustration.

It is also easy to detect an image volume with span disparity because the liver span of its scan profile is much shorter than that of its corresponding estimated liver profile. To differentiate between the two possible causes, the location of the discrepancy matters. If it happens at one end of the volume, with no additional image slices outside the scan profile's support, the cause can be determined to be a partial acquisition. Otherwise, it is a partial segmentation (Fig. 4).

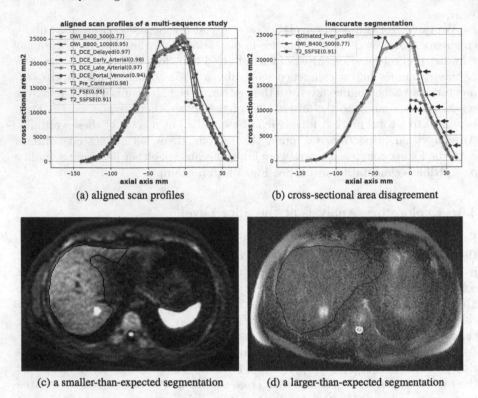

(a) aligned scan profiles

(b) cross-sectional area disagreement

(c) a smaller-than-expected segmentation

(d) a larger-than-expected segmentation

Fig. 3. (a) The aligned scan profiles of a study. A significant cross-sectional area disagreement between a scan profile and its estimated liver profile at the same axial axis location indicates a segmentation error. (b) The blue (DWI_B400_500) scan profile identifies a few slices with smaller than expected liver cross-sectional area (pointed by the red arrows) whereas the indigo (T2_SSFSE) scan profile suggests over-segmentation in multiple slices (pointed by the black arrows). For example, (c) (resp. (d)) Shows a detected slice with too small (resp. too large) a segmented area. Bad image quality seems to be responsible for the error in (d). (Color figure online)

The span disparity does not need to result in a low coherence score (Fig. 4a). It is independent of cross-sectional area disagreement in that one does not necessarily entail the other. But both can happen at the same time, too.

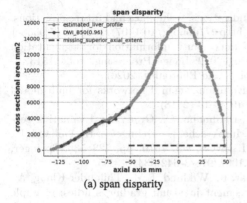
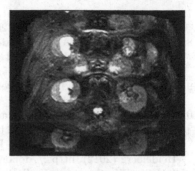

(a) span disparity   (b) cause of partial segmentation

Fig. 4. (a) Shows the span disparity of a scan profile with respect to its estimated liver profile. The red line represents the axial extent of the superior liver portion missing from this volume. Additional image slices do exist to the right the scan profile' support. But they suffer from severe artefacts and were not marked by the radiologists. (b) Shows one of these remaining slices. (Color figure online)

4   Conclusion

In this paper, based on the concept of liver profile, we have presented an exploratory data analysis approach to liver segmentation quality control for multi-sequence MR liver studies. Our method is efficient and allows to locate inaccurately segmented image slices.

Due to its mild assumptions, this method may also carry over to the analysis of segmented liver contours arising from multi-phase CT or longitudinal studies. Furthermore, it may also be applicable to assessing the segmentation quality of other anatomies in a similar context.

References

1. Balakrishnan, G., Zhao, A., Sabuncu, M.R., Guttag, J., Dalca, A.V.: VoxelMorph: a learning framework for deformable medical image registration. IEEE Trans. Med. Imaging **38**(8), 1788–1800 (2019)
2. Barrett, H.H., Myers, K.J., Hoeschen, C., Kupinski, M.A., Little, M.P.: Task-based measures of image quality and their relation to radiation dose and patient risk. Phys. Med. Biol. **60**(2), R1 (2015)
3. Bilic, P., et al.: The liver tumor segmentation benchmark (LiTS). arXiv preprint arXiv:1901.04056 (2019)
4. Chlebus, G., Schenk, A., Moltz, J.H., van Ginneken, B., Hahn, H.K., Meine, H.: Automatic liver tumor segmentation in CT with fully convolutional neural networks and object-based postprocessing. Sci. Rep. **8**(1), 1–7 (2018)
5. DeVries, T., Taylor, G.W.: Leveraging uncertainty estimates for predicting segmentation quality. arXiv preprint arXiv:1807.00502 (2018)
6. Esses, S.J., et al.: Automated image quality evaluation of T2-weighted liver MRI utilizing deep learning architecture. J. Magn. Reson. Imaging **47**(3), 723–728 (2018)

7. Gotra, A., et al.: Liver segmentation: indications, techniques and future directions. Insights Imaging 8(4), 377–392 (2017). https://doi.org/10.1007/s13244-017-0558-1
8. Hoebel, K., et al.: An exploration of uncertainty information for segmentation quality assessment. In: Medical Imaging 2020: Image Processing, vol. 11313, p. 113131K. International Society for Optics and Photonics (2020)
9. Hu, Y., et al.: Weakly-supervised convolutional neural networks for multimodal image registration. Med. Image Anal. 49, 1–13 (2018)
10. Kohlberger, T., Singh, V., Alvino, C., Bahlmann, C., Grady, L.: Evaluating segmentation error without ground truth. In: Ayache, N., Delingette, H., Golland, P., Mori, K. (eds.) MICCAI 2012, Part I. LNCS, vol. 7510, pp. 528–536. Springer, Heidelberg (2012). https://doi.org/10.1007/978-3-642-33415-3_65
11. Ledenius, K., Svensson, E., Stålhammar, F., Wiklund, L.M., Thilander-Klang, A.: A method to analyse observer disagreement in visual grading studies: example of assessed image quality in paediatric cerebral multidetector CT images. Br. J. Radiol. 83(991), 604–611 (2010)
12. Li, Z., Zhang, S., Zhang, J., Huang, K., Wang, Y., Yu, Y.: MVP-Net: multi-view FPN with position-aware attention for deep universal lesion detection. In: Shen, D., et al. (eds.) MICCAI 2019, Part VI. LNCS, vol. 11769, pp. 13–21. Springer, Cham (2019). https://doi.org/10.1007/978-3-030-32226-7_2
13. Ma, J.J., et al.: Diagnostic image quality assessment and classification in medical imaging: opportunities and challenges. In: 2020 IEEE 17th International Symposium on Biomedical Imaging (ISBI), pp. 337–340. IEEE (2020)
14. Roy, A.G., Conjeti, S., Navab, N., Wachinger, C.: Inherent brain segmentation quality control from fully convnet monte Carlo sampling. In: Frangi, A.F., Schnabel, J.A., Davatzikos, C., Alberola-López, C., Fichtinger, G. (eds.) MICCAI 2018. LNCS, vol. 11070, pp. 664–672. Springer, Cham (2018). https://doi.org/10.1007/978-3-030-00928-1_75
15. Sujit, S.J., Coronado, I., Kamali, A., Narayana, P.A., Gabr, R.E.: Automated image quality evaluation of structural brain MRI using an ensemble of deep learning networks. J. Magn. Reson. Imaging 50(4), 1260–1267 (2019)
16. Valindria, V.V., et al.: Reverse classification accuracy: predicting segmentation performance in the absence of ground truth. IEEE Trans. Med. Imaging 36(8), 1597–1606 (2017)
17. Vorontsov, E., Tang, A., Pal, C., Kadoury, S.: Liver lesion segmentation informed by joint liver segmentation. In: 2018 IEEE 15th International Symposium on Biomedical Imaging (ISBI 2018), pp. 1332–1335. IEEE (2018)
18. Yan, K., Wang, X., Lu, L., Summers, R.M.: DeepLesion: automated mining of large-scale lesion annotations and universal lesion detection with deep learning. J. Med. Imaging 5(3), 036501 (2018)

Pattern Analysis of Substantia Nigra in Parkinson Disease by Fifth-Order Tensor Decomposition and Multi-sequence MRI

Hayato Itoh[1]([✉]), Tao Hu[1], Masahiro Oda[1,2], Shinji Saiki[3], Koji Kamagata[3], Nobutaka Hattori[3], Shigeki Aoki[3], and Kensaku Mori[1,2,4,5]

[1] Graduate School of Informatics, Nagoya University, Nagoya, Japan
hitoh@mori.m.is.nagoya-u.ac.jp
[2] Information and Communications, Nagoya University, Nagoya, Japan
[3] School of Medicine, Juntendo University, Tokyo, Japan
[4] Information Technology Center, Nagoya University, Nagoya, Japan
[5] Research Center for Medical Bigdata, National Institute of Informatics, Tokyo, Japan

Abstract. This work proposes a new feature extraction method to analyse patterns of the substantia nigra in Parkinson disease. Recent imaging techniques such that neuromelanin-sensitive MRI enable us to recognise the region of the substantia nigra and capture early Parkinson-disease-related changes. However, automated feature extraction of Parkinson-disease-related changes and their geometrical interpretation are still challenging. To tackle these challenges, we introduce a fifth-order tensor expression of multi-sequence MRI data such as T1-weighted, T2-weighted, and neuromelanin images and its tensor decomposition. Reconstruction from the selected components of the decomposition visualises the discriminative patterns of the substantia nigra between normal and Parkinson-disease patients. We collected multi-sequence MRI data from 155 patients for experiments. Using the collected data, we validate the proposed method and analyse discriminative patterns in the substantia nigra. Experimental results show that the geometrical interpretation of selected features coincides with neuropathological characteristics.

Keywords: Parkinson disease · Substantia nigra · Multi-sequence data · Tensor decomopsition · Feature extraction · Image analysis

1 Introduction

Parkinson disease is the second most common progressive neurodegenerative disorder, with approximately 8.5 million people who had been affected worldwide in 2017 [1]. The characteristic of Parkinson disease is a progressive loss of dopaminergic neurons in the substantia nigra pars compacta [2]. Currently, the

X. Li et al. (Eds.): MMMI 2022, LNCS 13594, pp. 63–75, 2022.
https://doi.org/10.1007/978-3-031-18814-5_7

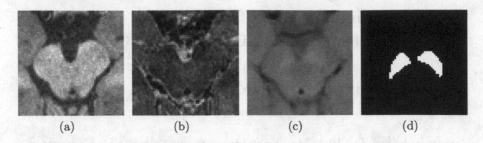

(a)   (b)   (c)   (d)

Fig. 1. Slices of volumetric images of three-type sequences. (a) T1WI. (b) T2WI. (c) NMI. (a)–(c) show the same region including substantia nigra of a normal patient. (d) G.T. for the region of the substantia nigra. By manual normalisation of intensities shown in (c), an expert neurologist can recognise the regions of the substantia nigra.

diagnosis of Parkinson disease depends on the clinical features acquired from patient history and neurological examination [3]. A traditional role of MRI for Parkinson disease is supporting clinical diagnosis by enabling the exclusion of other disease processes [4]. However, several advanced imaging markers have emerged as tools for the visualisation of neuro-anatomic and functional processes in Parkinson disease. As one of them, neuromelanin-sensitive MRI uses high-spatial-resolution T1-weighted imaging with fast spin-echo sequences at 3-Tesla MRI [5,6]. This new imaging technique provides a neuromelanin image (NMI) with neuromelanin-sensitive contrast, and T1 high-signal-intensity areas in the midbrain represent neuromelanin-rich areas. Since neuromelanin exists only in dopaminergic neurons of the substantia nigra pars compacta and noradrenergic neurons of locus coeruleus, NMI is useful for analysing the substantia nigra by capturing early Parkinson-disease-related changes. Figure 1 shows the examples of slice images of T1-weighted image (T1WI), T2-weighted image (T2WI), and NMI with annotation labels of the substantia nigra.

We propose a new feature-extraction method to analyse patterns of substantia nigra in Parkinson disease. For the analysis, we use T1WI, T2WI, and NMI. Even though only NMI is the valid imaging for recognising the region of the substantia nigra among these three, T1WI and T2WI help obtain anatomical information. In addition to anatomical information, a simple division of intensities of T1WI by ones of T2WI yields a new quantitative contrast, T1w/T2w ratio, with sensitivity to neurodegenerative changes [7]. A combination of different imaging sequences can offer more useful information for the analysis. Therefore, we use these multi sequences for our analysis. In developing a new feature extraction method, we set a triplet of volumetric images: T1WI, T2WI, and NMI to be a multi-sequence volumetric image for each patient. As the extension of a higher-order tensor expression of a set of volumetric images [8], we express a set of multi-sequence volumetric images by a fifth-order tensor expression shown in Fig. 2(a). Inspired by tensor-based analytical methods [9–11], we decompose this fifth-order tensor into a linear combination of fifth-order rank-1 tensors. By re-ordering the elements of this decomposition result, as shown in Fig. 2(b), we

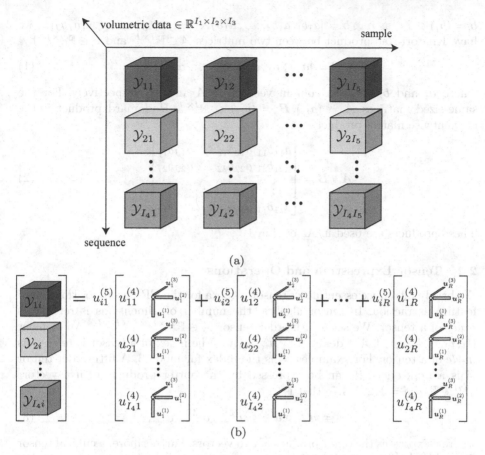

Fig. 2. Tensor expression and decomposition of multi-sequence volumetric images. (a) Fifth-order expression of a set of sampled multi-sequence volumetric images. (b) Decomposition of multi-sequence volumetric image.

obtain the decomposition of each multi-sequence volume image. This decomposition is a linear combination of fourth-order rank-1 tensors and their weights. Since this decomposition is based on the identical fourth-order rank-1 tensors, a set of weights expresses the characteristics of a multi-sequence volumetric image. Therefore, by selecting discriminative weights as feature vectors for normal and Parkinson disease, we achieve a feature extraction for analysing patterns of the substantia nigra between normal- and Parkinson-disease patients.

2   Mathematical Preliminary

2.1   Matrix Operations

We introduce two products of matrices since these are necessary for the CP-decomposition. Setting the Kronecker product of vectors $\boldsymbol{a} = (a_i) \in \mathbb{R}^I$ and

$b = (b_j) \in \mathbb{R}^J$ as $a \otimes b = [a_1b_1, a_1b_2, \ldots, a_1b_J, \ldots, a_{I-1}b_J, a_Ib_1, \ldots, a_Ib_J]^\top$, we have Khatori-Rao product between two matrices $\mathcal{A} \in \mathbb{R}^{I \times K}$ and $\mathcal{B} \in \mathbb{R}^{J \times K}$ by

$$A \odot B = [a_1 \otimes b_1, a_2 \otimes b_2, \ldots, a_K \otimes b_K], \tag{1}$$

where a_i and b_i are i-th column vectors of A and B, respectively. For the same-sized matrices $A = (a_{ij}), B = (b_{ij}) \in \mathbb{R}^{I \times J}$, Hadamard product is the elementwise matrix product

$$A * B = \begin{bmatrix} a_{11}b_{11} & a_{12}b_{12} & \cdots & a_{1J}b_{1j} \\ a_{21}b_{21} & a_{22}b_{22} & \cdots & a_{2J}b_{2j} \\ \vdots & \vdots & \ddots & \vdots \\ a_{I1}b_{I1} & a_{I2}b_{I2} & \cdots & a_{IJ}b_{Ij} \end{bmatrix}. \tag{2}$$

These products are used in Algorithm 1.

2.2   Tensor Expresstion and Operations

We briefly introduce essentials of tensor algebra for the CP-decomposition-based feature extraction. In tensor algebra, the number of dimensions is refered as *order* of a tensor. We set a fifth-order tensor $\mathcal{A} \in \mathbb{R}^{I_1 \times I_2 \times I_3 \times I_4 \times I_5}$. An element $(i_1, i_2, i_3, i_4, i_5)$ of $\mathcal{A}$ is denoted by $a_{i_1i_2i_3i_4i_5}$. The index of a tensor is refered as *mode* of a tensor. For examples, i_3 is the index for mode 3. A fifth-order tensor $\mathcal{A}$ is a rank one if it can be expressed by the ourter products of five vectors $u^{(j)} \in \mathbb{R}^{I_j}$, $j = 1, 2, 3, 4, 5$, that is

$$\mathcal{A} = u^{(1)} \circ u^{(2)} \circ u^{(3)} \circ u^{(4)} \circ u^{(5)}, \tag{3}$$

where $\circ$ expresses the outer product of two vectors. Furthermore, a cubical tensor $\mathcal{C} \in \mathbb{R}^{I \times I \times I \times I \times I}$ is diagonal if $a_{i_1i_2i_3i_4i_5} \neq 0$ only if $i_1 = i_2 = i_3 = i_4 = i_5$. We use $\boldsymbol{I}$ to denote the cubical identity tensor with ones of the superdiagonal and zeros elsewhere.

For two tensors $\mathcal{A}, \mathcal{B} \in \mathbb{R}^{I_1 \times I_2 \times I_3 \times I_4 \times I_5}$, we have the inner product

$$\langle \mathcal{A}, \mathcal{B} \rangle = \sum_{i_1=1}^{I_1} \sum_{i_2=1}^{I_2} \sum_{i_3=1}^{I_3} \sum_{i_4=1}^{I_4} \sum_{i_5=1}^{I_5} a_{i_1i_2i_3i_4i_5} b_{i_1i_2i_3i_4i_5}, \tag{4}$$

where $a_{i_1i_2i_3i_4i_5}$ and $b_{i_1i_2i_3i_4i_5}$ expresses elements of $\mathcal{A}$ and $\mathcal{B}$, respectively. This inner norm derives a norm of tensor

$$\|\mathcal{A}\| = \sqrt{\langle \mathcal{A}, \mathcal{A} \rangle} = \sqrt{\sum_{i_1=1}^{I_1} \sum_{i_2=1}^{I_2} \sum_{i_3=1}^{I_3} \sum_{i_4=1}^{I_4} \sum_{i_5=1}^{I_5} a_{i_1i_2i_3i_4i_5}^2}. \tag{5}$$

Unfolding of a tensor $\mathcal{A}$ is reshaping $\mathcal{A}$ by fixing one mode α. The α-mode unfolding gives a matrix $\mathcal{A}_{(\alpha)} \in \mathbb{R}^{I_\alpha \times (I_\beta I_\gamma I_\delta I_\epsilon)}$ for $\{\alpha, \beta, \gamma, \delta, \epsilon\} = \{1, 2, 3, 4, 5\}$. For a tensor and its unfoding, we have the bijection $\mathfrak{F}_{(n)}$ such that

$$\mathfrak{F}_{(n)}\mathcal{A} = \mathcal{A}_{(n)}, \quad \mathcal{A} = \mathfrak{F}_{(n)}^{-1}\mathcal{A}_{(n)}. \tag{6}$$

Algorithm 1: CP decomposition

Input: a fifth-order tensor $\mathcal{T}$, CP rank R, a sufficient small number ε
  the maximum number of iteration N

 initialise $U^{(n)} = [u_1^{(n)}, u_2^{(n)}, \ldots, u_R^{(n)}] \in \mathbb{R}^{I_n \times R}$ for $n = 1,2,3,4,5$

 for $i = 1, 2, \ldots, N$

  for $n = 1, 2, 3, 4, 5$

   Set $\{\alpha, \beta, \gamma, \delta\} = \{1,2,3,4,5\} \setminus n$ with a condtion $\alpha < \beta < \gamma < \delta$

   $V = U^{(\alpha)\top}U^{(\alpha)} * U^{(\beta)\top}U^{(\beta)} * U^{(\gamma)\top}U^{(\gamma)} * U^{(\delta)\top}U^{(\delta)}$

   Compute the Moore-Penrose pseudoinverse [15] of V as $V^\dagger$

   $U^{(n)} = \mathcal{T}_{(n)}(U^{(\delta)} \odot U^{(\gamma)} \odot U^{(\beta)} \odot U^{(\alpha)})V^\dagger$

  if $\|\mathcal{T} - \sum_{r=1}^{R} u_r^{(1)} \circ u_r^{(2)} \circ u_r^{(3)} \circ u_r^{(4)} \circ u_r^{(5)}\| \ll \varepsilon$

  break

Output: a set $\{U^{(n)}\}_{n=1}^5$ satisfying

  $\mathcal{T} \approx \underline{I} \times_1 U^{(1)} \times_2 U^{(2)} \times_3 U^{(3)} \times_4 U^{(4)} \times_5 U^{(5)}$

This n-mode unfolding derives n-mode product with a matrix $U^{(n)} \in \mathbb{R}^{J \times I_n}$

$$\mathcal{A} \times_n U^{(n)} = \mathfrak{F}_{(n)}^{-1}(U^{(n)} \mathcal{A}_{(n)}). \tag{7}$$

For elements $u_{ji_n}^{(n)}$ with $j = 1, 2, \ldots, J$ and $i_n = 1, 2, \ldots, I_n$ of $U^{(n)}$, we have

$$(\mathcal{A} \times_n U^{(n)})_{i_1 \ldots i_{n-1} j i_{n+1} \ldots i_5} = \sum_{i_n=1}^{I_n} a_{i_1 i_2 \ldots i_5} u_{ji_n}^{(n)}. \tag{8}$$

3 Feature Extraction for Multi-sequence Volumetric Data

We propose a new feature extraction method to analyse the difference of multi-sequence volumetric images between two categories. Setting $\mathcal{Y}_{i,1} \in \mathbb{R}^{I_1 \times I_2 \times I_3}$ for $j = 1, 2, \ldots, I_4$ to be volumetric images measured by different I_4 sequences for i-th sample, we have multi-sequence volumetric images as a fourth-order tensor $\mathcal{X}_i = [\mathcal{Y}_{i,1}, \mathcal{Y}_{i,2}, \ldots, \mathcal{Y}_{i,I_4}] \in \mathbb{R}^{I_1 \times I_2 \times I_3 \times I_4}$. We express multi-sequence volumetric data of I_5 samples by a fifth-order tensor $\mathcal{T} = [\mathcal{X}_1, \mathcal{X}_2, \ldots, \mathcal{X}_{I_5}] \in \mathbb{R}^{I_1 \times I_2 \times I_3 \times I_4 \times I_5}$ as shown in Fig. 2(a). In this expression, we assume that regions of interest are extracted with cropping and registration as the same-sized volumetric data via preprocessing. For $\mathcal{T}$, we compute CP decomposition [11,12]

$$\mathcal{T} = \sum_{r=1}^{R} u_r^{(1)} \circ u_r^{(2)} \circ u_r^{(3)} \circ u_r^{(4)} \circ u_r^{(5)} + \mathcal{E} \tag{9}$$

by minimising the norm $\|\mathcal{E}\|$ of a reconstruction error $\mathcal{E}$. In Eq. (9), a tensor is decomposed to R rank-1 tensors. Therefore, R is refered to as a CP rank. Algorithm 1 summarises the alternative reast square method [13,14] for CP decomposition.

From the result of Eq. (9), setting $u_{kr}^{(n)}$ is the k-th element of $\boldsymbol{u}_r^{(n)}$, we have reconstructed volumetric and multi-sequencel volumetric images by

$$\check{\mathcal{Y}}_{ji} = \sum_{r=1}^{R} u_{jr}^{(4)} u_{ir}^{(5)} (\boldsymbol{u}_r^{(1)} \circ \boldsymbol{u}_r^{(2)} \circ \boldsymbol{u}_r^{(3)}), \tag{10}$$

$$\check{\mathcal{X}}_{i} = \sum_{r=1}^{R} u_{ir}^{(5)} (\boldsymbol{u}_r^{(1)} \circ \boldsymbol{u}_r^{(2)} \circ \boldsymbol{u}_r^{(3)} \circ \boldsymbol{u}_r^{(4)}), \tag{11}$$

respectively. Figure 2(b) illustrates the visual interpretation of Eqs. (10) and (11). In these equations, rank-1 tensors $\boldsymbol{u}_r^{(1)} \circ \boldsymbol{u}_r^{(2)} \circ \boldsymbol{u}_r^{(3)}, r = 1, 2, \ldots, R$ express parts of patterns among all volumetric images in three-dimensional space. In Eq. (11), rank-1 tensors $(\boldsymbol{u}_r^{(1)} \circ \boldsymbol{u}_r^{(2)} \circ \boldsymbol{u}_r^{(3)} \circ \boldsymbol{u}_r^{(4)}), r = 1, 2, \ldots, R$ expresses parts of patterns among multi-sequence volumetric images. In Eq. (11), $u_{ri}^{(5)}$ indicates the importance of a part of patterns among multi-sequence data for i-th sample. Therefore, a set $u_{i11}^{(5)}, u_{i2}^{(5)}, \ldots, u_{iR}^{(5)}$ express features of multi-sequence pattern of i-th sample.

We select discriminative feature from the results of CP decomposition to analyse the difference between two categories. Setting C_1 and C_2 to be sets of indices of images for two categories, we have the means and variances of $u_{ir}^{(5)}$ by

$$\mu_r = \mathbb{E}(u_{ir}^{(5)}) \quad \text{and} \quad \sigma_r^2 = \mathbb{E}((u_{ir}^{(5)} - \mu_r)^2), \tag{12}$$

$$\mu_{1r} = \mathbb{E}(u_{ir}^{(5)} | i \in C_1) \quad \text{and} \quad \sigma_{1r}^2 = \mathbb{E}((u_{ir}^{(5)} - \mu_{1r})^2 | i \in C_1), \tag{13}$$

$$\mu_{2r} = \mathbb{E}(u_{ir}^{(5)} | i \in C_2) \quad \text{and} \quad \sigma_{2r}^2 = \mathbb{E}((u_{ir}^{(5)} - \mu_{2r})^2 | i \in C_2), \tag{14}$$

for all indices of i, C_1 and C_2, respectively. We set intra-class and inter-class variance by

$$\sigma_{\mathrm{B}r}^2 = \frac{N_1}{N}(\mu_{1r} - \mu_r)^2 + \frac{N_2}{N}(\mu_{2r} - \mu_r)^2, \tag{15}$$

$$\sigma_{\mathrm{W}r}^2 = \frac{N_1}{N}\sigma_{1r}^2 + \frac{N_2}{N}\sigma_{2r}^2, \tag{16}$$

respectively. Using Eqs. (15) and (16), we have seperability [16, 17] as

$$s_r = \frac{\sigma_{\mathrm{B}r}^2}{\sigma_{\mathrm{W}r}^2} = \frac{\sigma_{\mathrm{B}r}^2}{\sigma_r^2 - \sigma_{\mathrm{B}r}^2}. \tag{17}$$

Sorting $s_1, s_2, dots, S_R$ in desending order, we have a sorted index $\tilde{r}_1, \tilde{r}_2, \ldots, \tilde{r}_R$ satisfying $s_{\tilde{r}_1} \geq s_{\tilde{r}_2} \geq \cdots \geq s_{\tilde{r}_R}$ and $\{\tilde{r}_1, \tilde{r}_2, \ldots, \tilde{r}_R\} = \{1, 2, \ldots, R\}$. We select L elements from $\boldsymbol{u}_r^{(5)}, r = 1, 2, \ldots, R$ as $\boldsymbol{f}_i = [u_{i\tilde{r}_1}^{(5)}, u_{i\tilde{r}_2}^{(5)}, \ldots, u_{i\tilde{r}_L}^{(5)}]^\top \in \mathbb{R}^L$ for multi-sequence volumetric images of i-th sample. Since these L elements have large seperabilities among R features, these elements indicate discriminative patterns in multi-sequence volumetric images between two categories.

4   Experiments

To analyse patterns of the substantia nigra between normal and Parkinson-disease patients in multi-sequence volumetric images: T1WI, T2WI, and NMI, we collected 155 multi-sequence volumetric images of 73 normal and 82 Parkinson-disease patients in a single hospital. In each multi-sequence volumetric image, T2WI and NMI are manually registered to the coordinate system of T1WI. Furthermore, a board-certified radiologist with ten years of experience specialising in Neuroradiology annotated regions of substantia nigra in NMIs. Therefore, each multi-sequence image has a pixel-wise annotation of the substantia nigra.

As the preprocessing of feature extraction, we cropped the regions of interest (ROI) of the substantia nigra from T1WI, T2WI, and NMI by using the annotations. The size of T1WI and T2WI is $224 \times 300 \times 320$ voxels of the resolution of $0.8 \, \text{mm} \times 0.8 \, \text{mm} \times 0.8 \, \text{mm}$. The size of NMI is $512 \times 512 \times 14$ voxels of the resolution of $0.43 \, \text{mm} \times 0.43 \, \text{mm} \times 3.00 \, \text{mm}$. We registered NMI to the space of T1WI for the cropping of ROIs. Setting the centre of an ROI to be the centre of gravity in a substantia nigra's region, we expressed an ROI of each sequence as third-order tensors of $64 \times 64 \times 64$.

In each third-order tensor, after setting elements of the outer region of substantia nigra to be zero, we normalised all the elements of a third-order tensor in the range of $[0, 1]$.

We expressed these third-order tensors of three sequences for 155 patients by a fifth-order tensor $\mathcal{T} \in \mathbb{R}^{64 \times 64 \times 64 \times 3 \times 155}$ and decomposed it by Algorithm 1 for $R = 64, 155, 300, 1000, 2000, 4000, 6000$. For the computation, we used Python with CPU of Intel Xeon Gold 6134 3.20 GHz and main memory 192 GB. Figure 3(a) shows the computational time of the decompositions. Figure 3(b) shows the mean reconstruction error $\mathbb{E}\left[\|\mathcal{Y}_{ij} - \breve{\mathcal{Y}}_{ij}\| / \|\mathcal{Y}_{ij}\|\right]$ for each sequence. Figure 4 summarises examples of the reconstructed volumetric images. From each of the seven decomposition results, we extracted 100-dimensional feature vectors.

We checked each distributions of feature vectors for the seven sets of the extracted features. In feature extraction, we set C_1 and C_2 to be sets of indices for normal and Parkinson-disease categories, respectively. For the checking, setting $(\cdot, \cdot)$ and $\| \cdot \|_2$ to be the inner product of vectors and L_2 norm, we computed a cosine similarity $(\boldsymbol{f}, \boldsymbol{\mu}) / (\|\boldsymbol{f}\|_2 \|\boldsymbol{\mu}\|_2)$ between a feature vector $\boldsymbol{f} \in \{\boldsymbol{f}_i\}_{i=1}^{155}$ and the mean vector $\boldsymbol{\mu} = \mathbb{E}(\boldsymbol{f}_i | i \in C_1)$. The left column of Fig. 5 shows the distributions of the consine similarities. Furthermore, we mapped feature vectors from 100-dimensional space onto two-dimensional space by t-SNE [18], which approximately preserves the local topology among feature vectors in the original space. The right column of Fig. 5 shows the mapped feature vectors in a two-dimensional space.

Finally, we explored the geometrical interpretation of selected features. As shown in Fig. 6, some selected features have large magnitudes. We thought these large-magnitude features express important patterns for an image. Therefore, we multiplied these large magnitudes (approximately 10 to 20 of 100 features) by 0.7 as feature suppression and reconstructed images for CP decomposition of

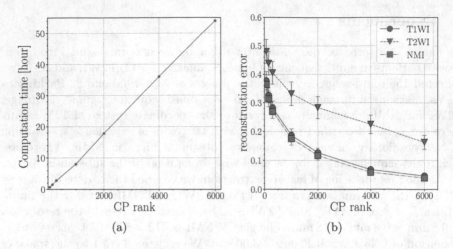

Fig. 3. Computational time and reconstruction error in CP decomposition. (a) Computational time against a CP rank. (b) Mean reconstruction errors of volumetric images against a CP rank. The mean reconstruction errors are computed for sequences: T1WI, T2WI, and NMI.

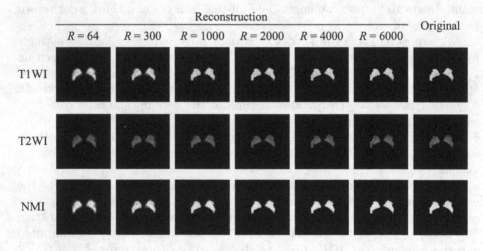

Fig. 4. Example slices of reconstructed and original multi-sequence volumetric images. The images express axial slices of reconstructed images for T1WI, T2WI, and NMI. R expresses a CP rank used in a CP decomposition.

$R = 6000$. By comparing these reconstructed multi-sequence volumetric images, we can observe important patterns corresponding to the suppressed features as not-reconstructed patterns. Figure 7 compares reconstructed multi-sequence volumetric images before and after the suppression of selected features.

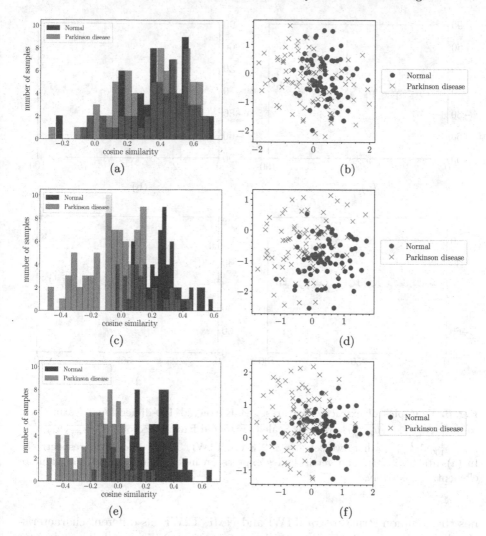

Fig. 5. Distribution of extracted feature vectors. Left column: Distribution of cosine similarities between a feature vector $f \in \{f_i\}_{i=1}^{155}$ and the mean vector $\mu = \mathbb{E}(f_i | i \in C_1)$. Right column: Visualisation of distribution of feature vectors. We map 100-dimensional feature vectors onto a two-dimensional space. In the top, middle, and bottom rows, we extracted 100-dimensional feature vectors from CP decompositions of $R = 1000, 4000$, and 6000, respectively.

5   Disucussion

In Fig. 3(b), the curves of mean reconstruction errors for T1WI and NMI are almost coincident, whilst the one of T2WI is different from these two. These results imply that intensity distributions on the substantia nigra between T1WI and NMI have similar structures. Even though the intensity distribution of T2WI

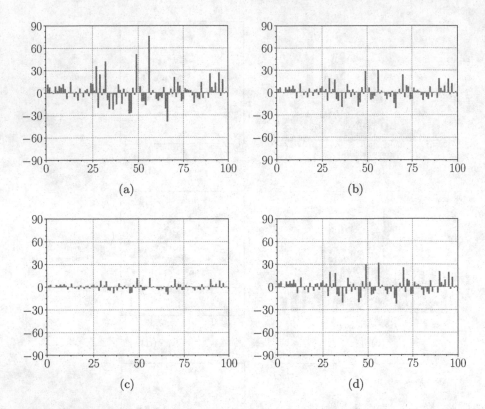

Fig. 6. Examples of extracted features. (a) Extracted 100-dimensional feature vector $[u_{i\tilde{r}_1}^{(5)}, u_{i\tilde{r}_2}^{(5)}, \ldots, u_{i\tilde{r}_{100}}^{(5)}]^\top$. (b)–(d) Scaled extracted feature vectors $[u_{j1}^{(4)}u_{i\tilde{r}_1}^{(5)}, u_{j2}^{(4)}u_{i\tilde{r}_2}^{(5)}, \ldots, u_{j100}^{(4)}u_{i\tilde{r}_{100}}^{(5)}]^\top$, where we set $j = 1, 2, 3$ for T1WI, T2WI, and NMI, respectively. In (a)–(d), horizontal and vertical axes express an index of an element and value of element, respectively.

has the common structure for T1WI and NMI, T2WI has different characteristics from these two. These characteristics are visualised in Fig. 4. Three images express shapes of substantia nigra, but the intensity distribution of T2WI are different from T1WI and NMI. Furthermore, Fig. 6(b)–(d) also indicate the same characteristics. In Fig. 6(b) and (d), the selected features for T1WI and NMI have similar distributions of elements, even though the one of T2WI has a different distribution.

In Fig. 4, the reconstruction of detail intensity distributions of multi-sequence volumetric images needs large R, while the blurred shape of the substantia nigra is captured even in small R such as 64, 300 and 1000. Since Algorithm 1 searches for rank-1 tensors to minimise reconstruction error by solving the least squares problems for each mode, the CP decomposition firstly captures common patterns among sequences and patients with a small number of rank-1 tensors. To obtain

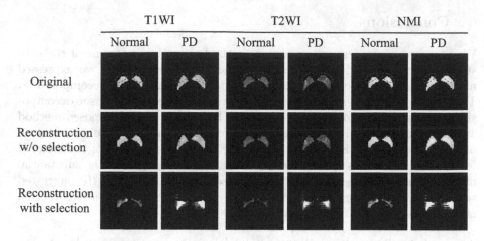

Fig. 7. Reconstruction with and without selected features. The top row shows the axial slices of the original multi-sequence volumetric images. In the top row, red dashed circles indicate the discriminative regions in multi-sequence volumetric images between normal and Parkinson disease. The middle row shows the axial slice of the reconstructed images from a CP decomposition of $R = 6000$. The bottom row shows the axial slices of reconstructed images for a CP decomposition of $R = 6000$, where we multiply the large feature values in selected 100 features by 0.7. (Color figure online)

rank-1 tensors expressing non-common patterns among the images, we have to increase the number of rank-1 tensors in the CP decomposition.

In Fig. 5(a), for normal and Parkinson disease, two distributions of cosine similarities almost overlap. This result shows that the selected features from the CP decomposition of $R = 1000$ are indiscriminative for two categories. As R increases in Fig. 5 (c) and (e), the overlap of the distributions between the two categories decreases. Figure 5(b), (d), and (f) also show the same characteristics as Fig. 5(a), (c), and (e). These results and the results in Fig. 4 imply that discriminative features between the two categories exist in non-common patterns with detailed local intensity distributions among multi-sequence volumetric images.

Figure 7 depicts the reconstructed images' missing regions after the suppression of selected features. Comparing the middle and bottom rows of Fig. 7, we observed the missing regions in specific parts of the substantia nigra. In the top row of Fig. 7, missing regions are marked on the original images by a red dashed circle. The marked regions include the regions of severe loss of neurons in Parkinson disease. The pars compacta of the substantia nigra is divided into ventral and dorsal tiers, and each tier is further subdivided into medial to lateral regions. In Parkinson disease, the ventrolateral tier of substantia nigra loses first, and then the ventromedial tier also loses. Typically the cells of 70–90% in the ventrolateral tier have been lost by the time a Parkinson-disease patient dies [19]. Since the missing regions include the ventrolateral tiers, we coluded that the proposed method achieved neuropathologically correct feature extraction.

6 Conclusions

We proposed a new feature extraction method to analyse patterns of the substantia nigra in Parkinson disease. For the feature extraction, we expressed multi-sequence volumetric images as a fifth-order tensor and decomposed it. The proposed method selects discriminative features from the tensor decomposition result. A series of experiments show the validity of the proposed method and important patterns in multi-sequence volumetric images for discrimination of Parkinson disease. Especially, our geometrical interpretation of the selected features in the visualisation clarified the discriminative region of the substantial nigra between normal and Parkinson-disease patients. Based on the suggested tensor-based pattern expression, we will explore an optimal feature-extraction method as a topic for future work.

Acknowledgements. Parts of this research were supported by the Japan Agency for Medical Research and Development (AMED, No. 22dm0307101h0004), and the MEXT/JSPS KAKENHI (No. 21K19898).

References

1. James, S.L., Abate, D., Abate, K.H., et al.: Global, regional, and national incidence, prevalence, and years lived with disability for 354 diseases and injuries for 195 countries and territories, 1990–2017: a systematic analysis for the global burden of disease study 2017. Lancet **392**(10159), 1789–1858 (2018)
2. Drui, G., Carnicella, S., Carcenac, C., Favier, M., et al.: Loss of dopaminergic nigrostriatal neurons accounts for the motivational and affective deficits in Parkinsons disease. Mol. Psychiatry **19**, 358–367 (2014)
3. Le Berre, A., et al.: Convolutional neural network-based segmentation can help in assessing the substantia nigra in neuromelanin MRI. Neuroradiology **61**(12), 1387–1395 (2019). https://doi.org/10.1007/s00234-019-02279-w
4. Bae, Y.J., Kim, J.-M., Sohn, C.-H., et al.: Imaging the substantia nigra in Parkinson disease and other Parkinsonian syndromes. Radiology **300**(2), 260–278 (2021)
5. Sasaki, M., Shibata, E., Tohyama, K., et al.: Neuromelanin magnetic resonance imaging of locus ceruleus and substantia nigra in Parkinson's disease. NeuroReport **17**(11), 1215–1218 (2006)
6. Kashihara, K., Shinya, T., Higaki, F.: Neuromelanin magnetic resonance imaging of nigral volume loss in patients with Parkinson's disease. J. Clin. Neurosci. **18**(8), 1093–1096 (2011)
7. Du, G., Lewis, M.M., Sica, C., Kong, L., Huang, X.: Magnetic resonance T1w/T2w ratio: a parsimonious marker for Parkinson disease. Ann. Neurol. **85**(1), 96–104 (2019)
8. Itoh, H., Imiya, A., Sakai, T.: Pattern recognition in multilinear space and its applications: mathematics, computational algorithms and numerical validations. Mach. Vis. Appl. **27**(8), 1259–1273 (2016). https://doi.org/10.1007/s00138-016-0806-2
9. Smilde, A., Bro, R., Geladi, P.: Multi-way Analysis: Applications in the Chemical Sciences, 1st edn. Wiley, Hoboken (2008)

10. Kroonenberg, P.M.: Applied Multiway Data Analysis, 1st edn. Wiley, Hoboken (2008)
11. Cichocki, A., Zdunek, R., Phan, A.H., Amari, S.: Nonnegative Matrix and Tensor Factorizations: Applications to Exploratory Multi-way Data Analysis and Blind Source Separation. Wiley, Hoboken (2009)
12. Kolda, T.G., Bader, B.W.: Tensor decompositions and applications. SIAM Rev. 51(3), 455–500 (2009)
13. Carroll, J., Chang, J.-J.: Analysis of individual differences in multidimensional scaling via an n-way generalization of Eckart-Young decomposition. Psychometrika 35(3), 283–319 (1970). https://doi.org/10.1007/BF02310791
14. Harshman, R.A.: Foundations of the PARAFAC procedure: models and conditions for an "explanatory" multi-model factor analysis. In: UCLA Working Papers in Phonetics, vol. 16, pp. 1–84 (1970)
15. Gollub, G.H., Lumsdaine, A.: Matrix Computation. Johns Hopkins University Press, Cambridge (1996)
16. Otsu, N.: A threshold selection method from gray-level histograms. IEEE Trans. Syst. Man Cybern. 9(1), 62–66 (1979)
17. Fukunaga, K.: Introduction to Statistical Pattern Recognition, 2nd edn. Academic Press, Cambridge (1990)
18. van der Maaten, L., Hinton, G.: Visualizing data using t-SNE. J. Mach. Learn. Res. 9, 2579–2605 (2008)
19. Ellison, E., et al.: Neuropathology. Mosby-Year Book, Maryland Heights (1998)

Gabor Filter-Embedded U-Net with Transformer-Based Encoding for Biomedical Image Segmentation

Abel A. Reyes[1] , Sidike Paheding[1]([✉]) , Makarand Deo[2],
and Michel Audette[3]

[1] Michigan Technological University, Houghton, MI 49931, USA
{areyesan,spahedin}@mtu.edu
[2] Norfolk State University, Norfolk, VA 23504, USA
mdeo@nsu.edu
[3] Old Dominion University, Norfolk, VA 23529, USA
maudette@odu.edu

Abstract. Medical image segmentation involves a process of categorization of target regions that are typically varied in terms of shape, orientation and scales. This requires highly accurate algorithms as marginal segmentation errors in medical images may lead to inaccurate diagnosis in subsequent procedures. The U-Net framework has become one of the dominant deep neural network architectures for medical image segmentation. Due to complex and irregular shape of objects involved in medical images, robust feature representations that correspond to various spatial transformations are key to achieve successful results. Although U-Net-based deep architectures can perform feature extraction and localization, the design of specialized architectures or layer modifications is often an intricate task. In this paper, we propose an effective solution to this problem by introducing Gabor filter banks into the U-Net encoder, which has not yet been well explored in existing U-Net-based segmentation frameworks. In addition, global self-attention mechanisms and Transformer layers are also incorporated into the U-Net framework to capture global contexts. Through extensive testing on two benchmark datasets, we show that the Gabor filter-embedded U-Net with Transformer encoders can enhance the robustness of deep-learned features, and thus achieve a more competitive performance.

Keywords: Gabor filters · Deep learning · U-Net · Vision transformers · Segmentation · Biomedical image

1 Introduction

Over the last decade, there has been a rapid development in the field of computer vision. Various tasks such as image segmentation, image classification and object detection have been drastically improved through the introduction of deep learning (DL) [1] architectures such as Convolutional Neural Networks (CNNs) [2,3].

© The Author(s), under exclusive license to Springer Nature Switzerland AG 2022
X. Li et al. (Eds.): MMMI 2022, LNCS 13594, pp. 76–88, 2022.
https://doi.org/10.1007/978-3-031-18814-5_8

The applications of DL techniques in the medical field are gaining popularity thanks to the impressive performance of end-to-end learning frameworks using raw image data [4,5]. In terms of biomedical image segmentation task, the U-Net [6], which is build upon Fully Convolutional Network (FCN) [7], has become a dominate architecture. The elegant representation of the U-Net architecture, consisting of decoder and encoder paths joined by a bridge layer, has inspired several variants [8–12] and has found numerous computer vision applications beyond the medical field [13–15]. Recently, the Transformer [16] and its variants have demonstrated exceptional performance in the field of Natural Language Processing (NLP). When comes to visual processing tasks, the Vision Transformer (ViT) [17], has gained popularity [18,19], including medical image segmentation [20,21]. Medical images, especially produced by magnetic resonance imaging (MRI), often are derived by several imaging protocols. Each protocol reveals different aspects of the same anatomy and hence they are complementary to each other. Since each modal image potentially addresses different clinical interpretations, it is often advantageous to exploit this multi-modal information. Several advanced filtering techniques have been used to extract image representation. One of the kinds is deformable filters [22], which is capable of enhancing the capacity to model geometric transformations, however, its increases the complexity of the model [23] and computational cost of the training. Another example of filtering methods is rotating filters. Zhou et al. [24] presented actively rotating filters where the filters rotate during convolutions to produce feature maps with explicit encoded location and orientation. However, this method has been proven to be more suitable for small and simple filters.

The Gabor filter [25] is one of the most popular in the field of image processing and computer vision [26,27]. Luan et al. showed [23] that Gabor filters exhibit some similarity with the learned filter in CNN [23]. And recent study showed that it can modulate the features learned and expand the network interpretability [28].

The contributions of this paper can be summarized as follows:

- To the best of our knowledge, this is the first work reporting the use of Gabor filters in a Transformer-based U-Net framework to enrich the feature representation for biomedical image segmentation.
- A new framework that embeds Gabor filter banks to a modified U-Net-based Transformer architecture in a late-fusion multi-modal approach is proposed.
- Extensive experiments are conducted on two benchmark datasets demonstrating outstanding performance of our proposed framework over several state-of-the-art segmentation architectures.

2   Related Works

There have been several studies that explored the use of Gabor filter characteristics in visual tasks. For instance, Gabor kernels were utilized to either initialize or serve as inputs in the DL models [29,30]. In the work presented by Luan et al. [23], Gabor filters were utilized in each layer to modulate the learned convolution filters in order to enhance the robustness in feature representation. Alekseev and Bobe [31] utilized Gabor filters in the first layer of their CNN design, making the parameters of the Gabor function learnable through standard backpropagation. Yuan et al. [32] introduced the use of adaptive Gabor Convolutional Networks, where the kernels on each CNN are adaptively multiplied by a bank of Gabor Filters, while the Gabor function parameters are constantly learned as convolutional kernels.

Recently, the use of Vision Transformers [17] for biomedical image segmentation has been explored. Chen et al. [20] proposed TransUNet, in which two popular architectures in computer vision: U-Net [6] and ViT are merged together. TransUNet leverages the Transformer's attention mechanisms to develop strong encoders, which eventually help to recover localized spatial information with the use of U-Net encoders. Yang et al. [33] proposed a new automated machine learning method which utilizing Transformers to optimize deep neural network architectures for lesion segmentation in 3D medical images. The results showed superior performance compared to the state-of-the-arts. Wang et al. [21] introduced an architecture that incorporates Transformers for biomedical volumetric image segmentation within a multi-modal approach, in which Transformers take the tokens from the encoder feature maps for global feature modeling. Finally, Chen et al. [34] addressed the problem of cross-modal interference by proposing a deep learning architecture, named OctopusNet, in which a different encoder is used for each modality, claiming to enhance feature extraction and avoiding feature explosion.

3   Methodology

In this work, we propose a new framework for medical image segmentation tasks. This framework has the following major contributions:

- Introduction of Gabor filter bank module to Transformer-encoded U-Net architectures.
- Incorporation of feature maps from the Gabor filters into multi-modal deep learning architectures for segmentation tasks.
- Development of a late fusion framework that consists of a Transformer encoder with multi-head self-attention based skip connections within a U-Net framework.

3.1   Gabor Filters

In computer vision, the use of different linear filtering techniques is widely accepted for image feature representation. Those techniques allow to leverage the unique characteristics found in a specific input image. Gabor filters [25], are wavelets (kernels) based on a sinusoidal plane wave with particular frequency and

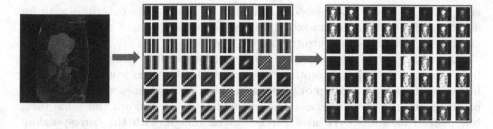

Fig. 1. Illustration of the Gabor filter banks applied to and MRI sample image.

orientation [26]. Theses filters are particularly used to model receptive fields. The wavelets are mathematically described as follows

$$g(x, y; \omega, \theta, \psi, \sigma, \gamma) = e^{\frac{-(x'^2 + \gamma^2 y'^2)}{2\sigma^2}} e^{(i(\omega x' + \psi))} \tag{1}$$

$$x' = x \cos\theta + y \sin\theta \tag{2}$$

$$y' = -x \cos\theta + y \cos\theta \tag{3}$$

where ω is represent the frequency $(2\pi/\lambda)$ of the wavelet's sinusoidal component, θ the orientation of the Gabor function's normal to the parallel stripes, ψ the phase offset and σ the standard deviation of the Gaussian envelope.

Gabor filters have proven to be a reliable tool to localize spatial and frequency domain properties, which make them a popular resource for various pattern analysis applications.

For this work, we extract features, through a set (bank) of Gabor filters, varying the parameters in such a way that the convolved outputs highlight embedded patterns and edges, within regions of interest. Figure 1 shows the resultant convoluted output from an MRI input layer with bank of Gabor filters, the outputs show a variety of edges highlighted according to the orientation provided by Gabor filters.

3.2 Transformers

Transformers were first proposed by Vaswami et al. [35] for Natural Language Processing (NLP). At a high level of understanding, the Transformer architecture consists of an embedding layer, an encoder and a decoder module. In the context of NLP, the embedding layer converts the collection of input words into a vector representation for each word, described as tokens within the architecture. Then, positional information is incorporated on each vector, known as positional encoding, in which global context is added as part of the embedding layer. The encoder module takes those vectors as input for the multi-head attention layers. At the end, all the outputs' heads are concatenated and passed through the multilayer perceptrons (MLP) as feed-forward neural network. This process can be repeated several times, since the several encoder layers can be stacked to boost the predictive power. The decoder consists of similarly computations with an additional process named masked multi-head attention, as well as an additional sub-layer which takes the output from the encoder.

Dosovitskiy et al. [17] extended the intuition behind Transformers to the field of computer vision. Essentially they analogize between words as tokens of large sentences with a group of pixels as a token of large images. These groups of pixels are known as patches. The embedding layer perform the same task, but instead of words, ViT uses patches of an image, with the corresponding positional information encoded. The embedding layer is then fed to the Transformer encoder which contains multi-head attention that integrates information globally. Multi-head attention is composed by a particular attention mechanism knowing as "Scaled Dot-Product Attention", which is mathematically described as

$$Attention(\mathbf{Q}, \mathbf{K}, \mathbf{V}) = softmax(\frac{\mathbf{Q}\mathbf{K}^T}{\sqrt{d_k}})\mathbf{V} \tag{4}$$

where $\mathbf{Q}$, $\mathbf{K}$, and $\mathbf{V}$ stand for queries, keys and values, respectively. The attention mechanism computes the dot-product of the queries with the keys, acting as an *attention filter*, which is scaled dividing by $\sqrt{d_k}$ (the dimension of $\mathbf{K}$). The softmax operation returns the weights that are multiplied against the values.

This attention function is repeated in parallel h times (h stands for heads), with different learned linear projections of $\mathbf{K}$, $\mathbf{Q}$, and $\mathbf{V}$ ($\mathbf{W}^Q, \mathbf{W}^K, \mathbf{W}^V$). These attention function outputs are concatenated and linearly projected with ($\mathbf{W}^O$). As a result, the multi-head attention network can be represented as:

$$Multihead(\mathbf{Q}, \mathbf{K}, \mathbf{V}) = Concat(h_1, .., h_i, .., h_h)\mathbf{W}^O \tag{5}$$

where

$$h_i = Attention(\mathbf{Q}\mathbf{W}_i^Q, \mathbf{K}\mathbf{W}_i^K, \mathbf{V}\mathbf{W}_i^V) \tag{6}$$

This attention mechanism is named as Multi-Head Self Attention.

3.3   GFT: Gabor Filters with Transformers

Figure 2 shows the proposed architecture which can be described as three different stages as follows.

The Gabor Filter Composite Stage: In this stage, each single modality is taken as input and is multiplied with a Gabor filter bank. The Gabor filter banks are determined prior by setting a range of parameters $(\lambda, \theta, \psi, \sigma, \gamma)$. Due to computational costs, the number of kernels in the Gabor filter bank is set as 24, obtained through the following set of parameters: $\lambda : \{\pi/4, \pi/2, 3\pi/4\}$; $\theta : \{0, \pi/4\}$; $\sigma : \{1, 3\}$; $\gamma : \{0.05, 0.5\}$; and $\psi : \{0\}$, with a kernel size of 9.

The U-Net-Based Transformer Architecture Stage: Inspired by the TransUNet architecture [20], in which Transformers are encoded in a U-Net architecture framework to leverage merits of CNN and transformers models. However, this architecture simply combines feature maps from encoder to decoder via

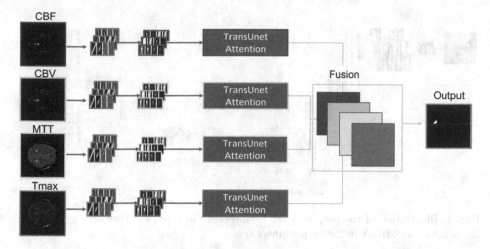

Fig. 2. Overall framework of the proposed methodology combining Gabor filters with Transformers for multimodal biomedical image segmentation.

skip connection without any operations, leading to a limited feature representation [36]. Therefore, in addition, and suggested by Attention U-Net [37], we add Multi-head Self Attention (MHSA) on each of the skip connection from the encoder to the decoder path in the TransUNet architecture to enrich the feature presentation. This addition leverages the spatial information granted in the early stages of the encoder path, thus helping to make the network contextualize better. Figure 3 illustrates the modified TransUnet architecture utilized in this proposed framework.

The Multi-modal Late-Fusion Output Stage: The last stage of the framework concatenates the outputs obtained using each modality as inputs, and computes dense layer operations to obtain a final pixel-wise classification to form an output segmentation mask. This work demonstrates the efficiency of combining each modality prediction's outcome separately to form a final prediction, instead of using all modalities at one combined input.

4 Results

4.1 Datasets

ISLES2018[1]. The ischemic stroke lesions segmentation (ISLES) challenge is a well known competition, holding a new edition every year since 2015 [38–40]. ISLES 2018 is composed by a total of six modalities: diffusion weighted imaging (DWI), computed tomography (CT), mean transit time (MTT), time to peak of te residue function (Tmax), cerebral blood flow (CBF) and cerebral blood volume (CBV). In this work, we utilize the training dataset provided by the

---

[1] http://www.isles-challenge.org/ISLES2018/.

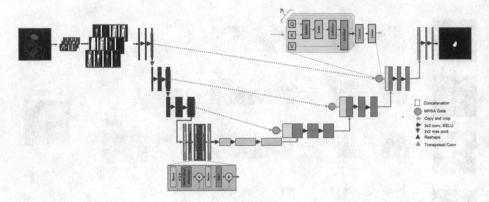

Fig. 3. Illustration of the proposed DL architecture inspired by TransUNet [20] with the addition of MHSA in the skip connections.

competition, since this dataset contains the larger number of cases (94) and each case is bundled with the corresponding ground truth segmentation mask required performance evaluation purpose. Each case contains 6 modalties (DWI, CT, Tmax, MTT, CBF and CBV) as volumes with the following dimension: $256 \times 256 \times n$, where n is the deep (or number of slices) for each volume, which varies in the range of 2 to 28 within this dataset. Since there is no uniformity among all the samples, therefore we separate each volume in layers and take them as input for the proposed multi-modal DL framework. In addition, the data set is split in a ratio of 8:2 for training and testing purpose correspondingly. During the training, a randomly selected 10% of the data is used for validation purpose. In order to reduce dimensionality and computational cost, we decide to use the four perfusion scan modalities provided (CBF, CBV. MTT, and Tmax) and discard the CT and DWI modalities for our analysis.

2018 Atrial Segmentation Challenge Dataset[2]. Opened in 2018, the Atrial Segmentation Challenge [41] addressed the detection of atrial fibrillation, since this is the most common type of cardiac arrhythmia. The data set is composed of 100 training samples and 54 testing samples, on both cases the ground truths are available for each sample of 3D late gadolinium-Enhanced Magnetic Resonance Imaging (LGE-MRI). In contrast to the ISLES 2018 dataset, each sample contains a total of 88 slices, however, the height and width differ from one sample to other (576×576 or 640×640), therefore we decide to resize each slide to 128×128 to keep uniformity on both training and testing sets.

4.2 Experimental Setup

All the experiments are set to be run in a Tesla A100 cluster GPU, for a total of 150 epochs, with a batch size of 16. The optimizer adopted for the set of experiments is Adam, with a learning schedule rate starting at 0.0001 and a decay factor of $e^{-0.01}$ every epoch. The best model is recorded every time the

[2] http://atriaseg2018.cardiacatlas.org/.

Table 1. Performance over the ISLES 2018 dataset.

	Evaluation metric			
	ACC	Dice	Jaccard	mIoU
U-Net (early-fusion)	0.8994	0.2378	0.1349	0.5164
U-Net (late-fusion)	0.9886	0.5332	0.3635	0.6760
Att. U-Net (early-fusion)	0.9369	0.3306	0.1980	0.5670
Att. U-Net (late-fusion)	0.9892	0.5605	0.3893	0.6892
UPEN (early-fusion)	0.9871	0.5820	0.4105	0.6988
UPEN (late-fusion)	0.9874	0.4147	0.2616	0.6245
TransUNet (early-fusion)	0.9554	0.3729	0.2291	0.5920
TransUNet (late-fusion)	**0.9894**	0.6190	0.4482	0.7188
GFT (early-fusion)	0.9753	0.5173	0.3489	0.6620
GFT (CBF)	0.9269	0.2776	0.1612	0.5435
GFT(CBV)	0.9860	0.5715	0.4001	0.6929
GFT (MTT)	0.9400	0.2939	0.1723	0.5558
GFT (Tmax)	0.9692	0.4831	0.3185	0.6436
GFT (late-fusion)	0.9873	**0.6417**	**0.4725**	**0.7299**

Table 2. Performance over the 2018 Atrial Segmentation Challenge dataset.

	Acc	Dice	Jaccard	mIoU
U-Net	0.9970	0.8961	0.8118	0.9043
Att. U-Net	0.9968	0.8897	0.8013	0.8990
UPEN	0.9971	0.9001	0.8184	0.9077
TransUNet	0.9971	0.9002	0.8186	0.9078
GFT	**0.9972**	**0.9044**	**0.8256**	**0.9114**

validation performance is improved, with a tolerance of 10 epochs for an early stop. For robustness of the result, during the training process, the dataset is randomly split in a ration of 9:1, for training and validation purpose, respectively.

4.3 Experimental Results

We first conduct experiments on the training set from the ISLES 2018 dataset. Our proposed framework achieves mean Intersection over Union (mIoU) of 0.5435, 0.6929, 0.5558 and 0.6436 for CBF, CBV, MTT and Tmax individual modalities, respectively. These results are competitive in comparison with state-of-the-art architectures for segmentation tasks such as U-Net [6], Attention U-Net [8], UPEN net [9] and TransUNet [20], when the input are taken without split them by each modality. Our proposed late fusion model outperforms the aforementioned biomedical image segmentation methods by achieving a mIoU of

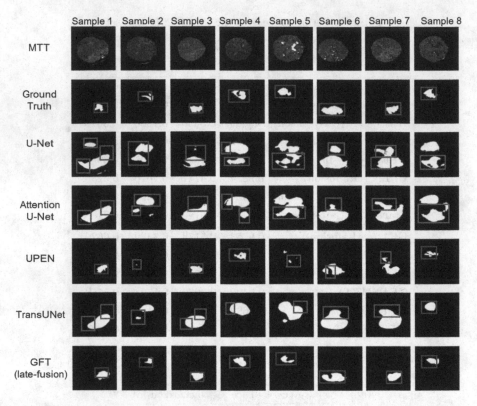

Fig. 4. The visual comparison of segmentation outputs on the ISLES 2018 dataset. Green boxes: location of true positive predictions. Red boxes: locations of false positive predictions. (Color figure online)

0.7299. Detailed quantitative results using the ISLES 2018 dataset are provided in Table 1. Figure 4 shows a visual comparison of segmentation results, the green boxes indicates the location of the segmentation mask, some methods as U-Net, Attention U-Net and TransUNet predict the region of interests along with some other areas (red boxes) that are not included in the ground truth. Techniques as UPEN, in the other hand, tends to be more accurate in the location of the segmentation mask, however in some samples also includes several false positives. In contrast our method shows prediction outputs much more alike the ground truth provided in the dataset, in both locations and segmentation shape.

In addition, we evaluate the performance of our proposed framework with the 2018 Atrial Segmentation Challenge dataset, since this dataset is just composed by one modality (LGE-MRI), there was not need to implement a multimodal approach. Our GFT approach achieves a mIoU of 0.9114, showing a solid superiority over the competing architectures. Our GFT also yields better performance in terms of accuracy, Dice score, and Jaccard coefficient. Details of the obtained results are summarized in Table 2. Figure 5 shows a visual comparison of segmentation results obtained from the aforementioned methods.

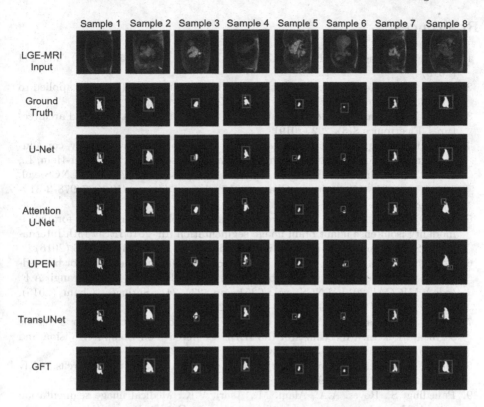

Fig. 5. The visual comparison of segmentation results on the 2018 Atrial Segmentation Challenge dataset.

5 Conclusions

We presented a new framework for biomedical image segmentation tasks, in which Gabor filters are introduced to leverage intrinsic feature representations from the different modalities in a volumetric sample of information. The proposed framework complement the rich feature representation obtained by the Gabor filters with a modified U-Net-based Transformer architecture. The extensive experiments performed on two well-known benchmark datasets showed that Gabor filter with Transformers outperformed different state-of-the-art architectures in terms of Dice score, mIoU, and Jaccard coefficient. Future work will be focused on the development of automatic selection for Gabor filter parameters $(\theta, \psi, \lambda, \sigma, \gamma)$ to produce an optimized Gabor filter bank and thus improve overall performance of the proposed architecture.

References

1. LeCun, Y., Bengio, Y., Hinton, G.: Deep learning. Nature **521**(7553), 436–444 (2015)
2. LeCun, Y., Bottou, L., Bengio, Y., Haffner, P.: Gradient-based learning applied to document recognition. Proc. IEEE **86**(11), 2278–2324 (1998)
3. Alom, M.Z., et al.: A state-of-the-art survey on deep learning theory and architectures. Electronics **8**(3), 292 (2019)
4. Shen, H., Wang, R., Zhang, J., McKenna, S.J.: Boundary-aware fully convolutional network for brain tumor segmentation. In: Descoteaux, M., Maier-Hein, L., Franz, A., Jannin, P., Collins, D.L., Duchesne, S. (eds.) MICCAI 2017. LNCS, vol. 10434, pp. 433–441. Springer, Cham (2017). https://doi.org/10.1007/978-3-319-66185-8_49
5. Nie, D., Wang, L., Gao, Y., Shen, D.: Fully convolutional networks for multi-modality isointense infant brain image segmentation. In: 2016 IEEE 13th International Symposium on Biomedical Imaging (ISBI), pp. 1342–1345. IEEE (2016)
6. Ronneberger, O., Fischer, P., Brox, T.: U-Net: convolutional networks for biomedical image segmentation. In: Navab, N., Hornegger, J., Wells, W.M., Frangi, A.F. (eds.) MICCAI 2015. LNCS, vol. 9351, pp. 234–241. Springer, Cham (2015). https://doi.org/10.1007/978-3-319-24574-4_28
7. Long, J., Shelhamer, E., Darrell, T.: Fully convolutional networks for semantic segmentation. In: Proceedings of the IEEE Conference on Computer Vision and Pattern Recognition, pp. 3431–3440 (2015)
8. Oktay, O., et al.: Attention U-Net: learning where to look for the pancreas. arXiv preprint arXiv:1804.03999 (2018)
9. Paheding, S., Reyes, A.A., Alam, M., Asari, V.K.: Medical image segmentation using U-Net and progressive neuron expansion. In: Pattern Recognition and Tracking XXXIII, vol. 12101, p. 1210102. SPIE (2022)
10. Alom, M.Z., Hasan, M., Yakopcic, C., Taha, T.M., Asari, V.K.: Recurrent residual convolutional neural network based on U-Net (R2U-Net) for medical image segmentation. arXiv preprint arXiv:1802.06955 (2018)
11. Siddique, N., Paheding, S., Alom, M.Z., Devabhaktuni, V.: Recurrent residual U-Net with efficientnet encoder for medical image segmentation. In: Pattern Recognition and Tracking XXXII, vol. 11735, pp. 134–142. SPIE (2021)
12. Siddique, N., Paheding, S., Elkin, C.P., Devabhaktuni, V.: U-Net and its variants for medical image segmentation: a review of theory and applications. IEEE Access **9**, 82031–82057 (2021)
13. Paheding, S., Reyes, A.A., Kasaragod, A., Oommen, T.: GAF-NAU: Gramian angular field encoded neighborhood attention U-Net for pixel-wise hyperspectral image classification. In: Proceedings of the IEEE/CVF Conference on Computer Vision and Pattern Recognition, pp. 409–417 (2022)
14. Soares, L.P., Dias, H.C., Grohmann, C.H.: Landslide segmentation with U-Net: evaluating different sampling methods and patch sizes. arXiv preprint arXiv:2007.06672 (2020)
15. McGlinchy, J., Johnson, B., Muller, B., Joseph, M., Diaz, J.: Application of UNet fully convolutional neural network to impervious surface segmentation in urban environment from high resolution satellite imagery. In: 2019 IEEE International Geoscience and Remote Sensing Symposium, IGARSS 2019, pp. 3915–3918. IEEE (2019)

16. Devlin, J., Chang, M.-W., Lee, K., Toutanova, K.: BERT: pre-training of deep bidirectional transformers for language understanding. arXiv preprint arXiv:1810.04805 (2018)

17. Dosovitskiy, A., et al.: An image is worth 16 × 16 words: transformers for image recognition at scale. arXiv preprint arXiv:2010.11929 (2020)

18. Touvron, H., Cord, M., Douze, M., Massa, F., Sablayrolles, A., Jégou, H.: Training data-efficient image transformers & distillation through attention. In: International Conference on Machine Learning, pp. 10347–10357. PMLR (2021)

19. Carion, N., Massa, F., Synnaeve, G., Usunier, N., Kirillov, A., Zagoruyko, S.: End-to-end object detection with transformers. In: Vedaldi, A., Bischof, H., Brox, T., Frahm, J.-M. (eds.) ECCV 2020. LNCS, vol. 12346, pp. 213–229. Springer, Cham (2020). https://doi.org/10.1007/978-3-030-58452-8_13

20. Chen, J., et al.: TransUNet: transformers make strong encoders for medical image segmentation. arXiv preprint arXiv:2102.04306 (2021)

21. Wang, W., Chen, C., Ding, M., Yu, H., Zha, S., Li, J.: TransBTS: multimodal brain tumor segmentation using transformer. In: de Bruijne, M., et al. (eds.) MICCAI 2021. LNCS, vol. 12901, pp. 109–119. Springer, Cham (2021). https://doi.org/10.1007/978-3-030-87193-2_11

22. Dai, J., et al.: Deformable convolutional networks. In: Proceedings of the IEEE International Conference on Computer Vision, pp. 764–773 (2017)

23. Luan, S., Chen, C., Zhang, B., Han, J., Liu, J.: Gabor convolutional networks. IEEE Trans. Image Process. **27**(9), 4357–4366 (2018)

24. Zhou, Y., Ye, Q., Qiu, Q., Jiao, J.: Oriented response networks. In: Proceedings of the IEEE Conference on Computer Vision and Pattern Recognition, pp. 519–528 (2017)

25. Gabor, D.: Theory of communication. Part 1: The analysis of information. J. Inst. Electr. Eng.-Part III: Radio Commun. Eng. **93**(26), 429–441 (1946)

26. Jain, A.K., Ratha, N.K., Lakshmanan, S.: Object detection using Gabor filters. Pattern Recogn. **30**(2), 295–309 (1997)

27. Kwolek, B.: Face detection using convolutional neural networks and Gabor filters. In: Duch, W., Kacprzyk, J., Oja, E., Zadrożny, S. (eds.) ICANN 2005. LNCS, vol. 3696, pp. 551–556. Springer, Heidelberg (2005). https://doi.org/10.1007/11550822_86

28. Gong, X., Xia, X., Zhu, W., Zhang, B., Doermann, D., Zhuo, L.: Deformable Gabor feature networks for biomedical image classification. In: Proceedings of the IEEE/CVF Winter Conference on Applications of Computer Vision, pp. 4004–4012 (2021)

29. Ouyang, W., Wang, X.: Joint deep learning for pedestrian detection. In: Proceedings of the IEEE International Conference on Computer Vision, pp. 2056–2063 (2013)

30. Zhang, B., Yang, Y., Chen, C., Yang, L., Han, J., Shao, L.: Action recognition using 3D histograms of texture and a multi-class boosting classifier. IEEE Trans. Image Process. **26**(10), 4648–4660 (2017)

31. Alekseev, A., Bobe, A.: GaborNet: Gabor filters with learnable parameters in deep convolutional neural network. In: 2019 International Conference on Engineering and Telecommunication (EnT), pp. 1–4. IEEE (2019)

32. Yuan, Y., et al.: Adaptive Gabor convolutional networks. Pattern Recogn. **124**, 108495 (2022)

33. Yang, D., Myronenko, A., Wang, X., Xu, Z., Roth, H.R., Xu, D.: T-AutoML: automated machine learning for lesion segmentation using transformers in 3D medical

imaging. In: Proceedings of the IEEE/CVF International Conference on Computer Vision, pp. 3962–3974 (2021)

34. Chen, Yu., Chen, J., Wei, D., Li, Y., Zheng, Y.: OctopusNet: a deep learning segmentation network for multi-modal medical images. In: Li, Q., Leahy, R., Dong, B., Li, X. (eds.) MMMI 2019. LNCS, vol. 11977, pp. 17–25. Springer, Cham (2020). https://doi.org/10.1007/978-3-030-37969-8_3

35. Vaswani, A., et al.: Attention is all you need. In: Advances in Neural Information Processing Systems, vol. 30 (2017)

36. Wang, B., Dong, P., et al.: Multiscale transunet++: dense hybrid U-Net with transformer for medical image segmentation. Signal Image Video Process. **16**, 1607–1614 (2022). https://doi.org/10.1007/s11760-021-02115-w

37. Wang, S., Li, L., Zhuang, X.: AttU-Net: attention U-Net for brain tumor segmentation. In: Crimi, A., Bakas, S. (eds.) BrainLes 2021, vol. 12963, pp. 302–311. Springer, Cham (2022). https://doi.org/10.1007/978-3-031-09002-8_27

38. Cereda, C.W., et al.: A benchmarking tool to evaluate computer tomography perfusion infarct core predictions against a DWI standard. J. Cereb. Blood Flow Metab. **36**(10), 1780–1789 (2016)

39. Hakim, A., et al.: Predicting infarct core from computed tomography perfusion in acute ischemia with machine learning: lessons from the isles challenge. Stroke **52**(7), 2328–2337 (2021)

40. Maier, O., et al.: ISLES 2015-a public evaluation benchmark for ischemic stroke lesion segmentation from multispectral MRI. Med. Image Anal. **35**, 250–269 (2017)

41. Xiong, Z.: A global benchmark of algorithms for segmenting the left atrium from late gadolinium-enhanced cardiac magnetic resonance imaging. Med. Image Anal. **67**, 101832 (2021)

Learning-Based Detection of MYCN Amplification in Clinical Neuroblastoma Patients: A Pilot Study

Xiang Xiang[1]([✉]), Zihan Zhang[1], Xuehua Peng[2], and Jianbo Shao[2]

[1] School of Artificial Intelligence and Automation, Huazhong University of Science and Technology, Wuhan, China
[2] Wuhan Children's Hospital Affiliated with Tongji Medical College, Huazhong University of Science and Technology, Wuhan, China
xex@hust.edu.cn

Abstract. Neuroblastoma is one of the most common cancers in infants, and the initial diagnosis of this disease is difficult. At present, the MYCN gene amplification (MNA) status is detected by invasive pathological examination of tumor samples. This is time-consuming and may have a hidden impact on children. To handle this problem, in this paper, we present a pilot study by adopting multiple machine learning (ML) algorithms to predict the presence or absence of MYCN gene amplification. The dataset is composed of retrospective CT images of 23 neuroblastoma patients. Different from previous work, we develop the algorithm without manually segmented primary tumors which is time-consuming and not practical. Instead, we only need the coordinate of the center point and the number of tumor slices given by a subspecialty-trained pediatric radiologist. Specifically, CNN-based method uses pre-trained convolutional neural network, and radiomics-based method extracts radiomics features. Our results show that CNN-based method outperforms the radiomics-based method.

Keywords: Neuroblastoma · MYCN amplification · CT · Radiomics · Convolutional neural network

1 Introduction

Neuroblastoma is one of the most common extracranial solid tumors in infant patients [1]. Despite a variety of treatment options, patients with high-risk neuroblastoma tend to have poor prognoses and low survival. MYCN gene amplification (MNA) is detected in 20% to 30% of neuroblastoma patients [2]. MNA is an important part of the neuroblastoma risk stratification system. It has been proved to be an independent predictor and is related to aggressive tumor behavior and poor prognosis [3]. The MYCN gene with higher amplification multiple

---

X. Xiang—Also with the Key Laboratory of Image Processing and Intelligent Control, Ministry of Education, China.

X. Li et al. (Eds.): MMMI 2022, LNCS 13594, pp. 89–97, 2022.
https://doi.org/10.1007/978-3-031-18814-5_9

indicates that the neuroblastoma may be a more invasive type and its prognosis may be worse. Therefore, MNA patients of any age are "high-risk" groups [1], and the detection of MNA is an essential part of the evaluation and treatment interventions of neuroblastoma.

MYCN gene amplification status is generally detected by invasive pathological examination of tumor samples which is time-consuming and may have a hidden impact on children. Therefore, it is significant to develop a fast and non-invasive method to predict the presence or absence of MNA.

Radiomics [4] is a method to rapidly extract innumerable quantitative features from tomographic images. This allows the transformation of medical image data into high-dimensional feature data. Radiomics is composed of a set of first-order, second-order, and higher-order statistical features on images. Previous studies [6–8] have shown significant relationships between image features and tumor clinical features. For example, Wu et al. [6] first segment primary tumors and extract radiomics features automatically from the ROI. An ML model is then trained with selected features.

Convolutional neural networks (CNN) are under-explored in the prediction of outcomes in neuroblastoma patients. CNN has shown incredible success in image classification tasks [9], and it is a potential approach for processing medical images. Although CNN is primarily driven by large-scale data, transfer learning has shown its effectiveness in training models with small amounts of data [10]. The number of our CT data is limited, and we use a pre-trained CNN model to handle the challenge of lack of medical image data.

In this work, we investigate the radiomics-based method and CNN-based method on a limited dataset. Specifically, we feed radiomics features into multiple ML models to predict the status of MNA. For CNN-based method, we use pre-trained ResNet [5] to extract deep features and predict the label of the data end-to-end. To the best of our knowledge, our method is the first study to try to simplify the annotation process. Specifically speaking, we do not need a pediatric radiologist to manually segment primary tumors which is time-consuming and not practical in clinical applications. Instead, we only need a pediatric radiologist to point out the center point of the tumor and the number of tumor slices in CT images. We crop the ROI images with fixed size and feed them into the model to predict the MNA status. This can greatly reduce the evaluation time of new CT data. Our results demonstrate comparable performance of previous segment-tumor method.

In summary, the contribution of this paper are as follows.

- We propose a novel CNN-based method to predict the presence or absence of MYCN gene amplification of the CT images.
- We greatly simplify the annotation process which makes the prediction process fast and practical, and we have achieved comparable performance with previous works while the evaluation time is greatly reduced.

In the following, we first review related work and the clinical data preparation, then elaborate on radiomics-based and CNN-based methods, and further empirically compare them, with a tentative conclusion followed in the end.

2   Related Work

There is an increasing interest in the prediction of patient outcomes based on medical images [16–21]. Wang et al. [11] propose a CNN-based method to predict the EGFR mutation status by CT scanning of lung adenocarcinoma patients. By training on a large number of CT images, the deep learning models achieve better predictive performance in both the primary cohort and the independent validation cohort. Wu et al. [6] combine clinical factors and radiomics features which are extracted from the manually delineated tumor. The combined model can predict the MNA status well. However, the annotation process makes the evaluation time-consuming. When evaluating new patient images, the method has to annotate the tumor ROI at first. Similarly [6], Liu et al. [7] extract radiomics feature from tumor ROI and apply pre-trained VGG model to extract CNN-based feature. Angela et al. [12] sketch the ROI on the CT images of neuroblastoma, then extract the radiomics features on ROI. With the extracted feature, they develop the radiology model after feature selection to predict the MNA status.

3   Clinical Data Preparation

Dataset. From the medical records, a total of 23 patients with pretreatment CT scans who have neuroblastoma are selected. Each patient has three-phase CT images. Inclusion criteria are (1) age ≤ 18 years old at the time of diagnosis, and (2) histopathologically confirmed MNA status detection. The number of presence of MNA in the enrolled patients is only two. The rest 21 patients do not have MNA.

Data Preprocessing. As shown in Fig. 1, the unit of measurement in CT scans is the Hounsfield Unit (HU). We first transform it into the gray level. In the CT scans, a pixel spacing may be [2.5, 0.5, 0.5], which means that the distance between slices is 2.5 mm. And the pixel spacing of different CT scans may vary. As a result, we resample the full dataset to a certain isotropic resolution. Then we transfer the CT scans into image format.

The proportion of MNA and non-MNA in the training cohort is highly imbalanced (2:21). The imbalance harms the generalizability and fairness of the model [15]. To tackle this problem, we adopt re-sampling method to augment the MNA CT image data. Specifically, we apply rotation, flipping, noise injection, and gamma calibration transformation techniques to CT images. For non-MNA images, we randomly select transformation techniques to augment the images, and for MNA images, we apply all transformation techniques to balance the dataset.

With the annotation information, we use a fixed-size filter (128 × 128 size) to crop the tumor out of each slice image around the center point of the tumor, and the cropped slice number is identical to the annotated tumor slice number. That ensures the extracted features correspond to the same spatial information across all images.

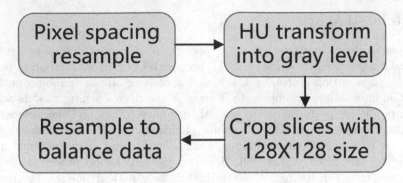

Fig. 1. The pre-processing of the CT data.

4 Proposed Methods

4.1 Radiomics-Based Method

As shown in Fig. 2, primary tumors are annotated from initial staging CT scans using open-source software package ITK-SNAP [13] by a subspecialty-trained pediatric radiologist. We use pyradiomics [14] to extract radiomics features, which is implemented based on consensus definitions of the Imaging Biomarkers Standardization Initiative (IBSI). We extract three kinds of radiomics features as shown in Table 1, 107 features in total. In summary, the first-order statistical features capture the intensity of the images. The shape features describe the geometric shape of the tumor. In our setting, the shape of the tumor is a cube (we do not precisely segment the tumor ROI), which may make the feature not separable because each tumor shape is similar. The gray level features represent the spatial relationship of the voxels.

After the feature extraction, we select the features which are highly correlated to the label. In specific, we apply LASSO linear regression to select the proper features, which reduces the dimension of the data and the number of features and it attenuates over-fitting. Note that we only apply the LASSO linear regression on the training set excluding the test set to prevent data leakage.

Finally, We adopt multiple ML methods to predict the MNA status including SVM, logistic regression, KNN, random forest and AdaBoost. The selected features and the label are the input of the model, and we train the model on CT images of 18 patients while other CT images are used for validation. We use stratified four-fold outer cross-validation to analyze the performance of our models. Note that the slices belonging to one patient could only b divided into training or test set, preventing slices of the same subject are used both for training and testing which invalidates the results.

4.2 CNN-Based Method

ResNet is widely used in computer vision. We adopt ResNet34 which is pre-trained on ImageNet to predict patient MNA status end-to-end from the CT

Table 1. Extracted radiomics features

First-order statistics	Shape-based	Gray level
Range	2D shape features	GLCM
Maximum		GLDM
Minimum	3D shape features	GLRLM
Mean		GLSZM
Variance		NGTDM
Total 18	Total 14	Total 75

images. We retrain the final layer of ResNet34 to predict the MNA status. To fit in the input size of the model, we crop the images into 128×128 size based on the center point of the tumor to ensure the tumor is at the center of the cropped images. The CT images are gray images while the model requires RGB images which are three-channel. We study three approaches to transform gray images into three-channel images. In specific, the first approach inputs the gray images into the model. The second approach transforms identical gray images into three-channel images. The third approach transforms gray images of adjacent slices into three-channel images.

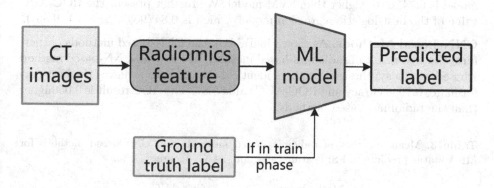

Fig. 2. Illustration of radiomics-based method process.

5 Experiments

We compare the performance of radiomics-based ML methods and CNN-based methods on our dataset.

Table 2. Accuracy of machine learning models for MNA status prediction. The number in brackets is the variance and the outer number is the mean of four-fold cross-validation accuracy. The best ROC-AUC value is 0.84 (95% CI: (0.81, 0.86))

ML methods	Accuracy
SVM	0.73 (±0.11)
Logistic regression	**0.74 (±0.11)**
KNN	0.72 (±0.09)
Random forest	0.71 (±0.09)
AdaBoost	0.70 (±0.12)

5.1 Experimental Results

For all experiments, we split the dataset into training set and validation set and do four-fold cross-validation. The training set contains 18 patients CT images while the validation set contains 5 patients CT images. The accuracy is reported on the total validation set images.

Radiomics-Based Methods. Among the ML techniques we experiment with, logistic regression model over radiomics features outperforms other models predicting MNA status as shown in Table 2. The mean accuracy of logistic regression model is 0.74, 0.01 higher than SVM model. We further present the ROC-AUC value of the best logistic regression model, which is 0.84 (95% CI: (0.81, 0.86)).

CNN-Based Methods. As shown in Table 3, the CNN-based methods outperform the best result of radiomics-based method. The second CNN-based method whose input is synthesized by three identical gray images achieves the best performance 0.79 accuracy and ROC-AUC value 0.87. The ACC result is 0.05 higher than the radiomics-based methods.

Table 3. Mean accuracy of radiomics-based methods and CNN-based methods for MNA status prediction. FS: Feature Selection. ACC: accuracy

Methods-based	ACC	AUC
Radiomics-based	0.72	0.81
FS + Radiomics-based	0.74	0.84
1_{st} CNN-based	0.73	0.85
2_{nd} CNN-based	**0.79**	**0.87**
3_{rd} CNN-based	0.73	0.83

5.2 Discussion

In this study, we investigate multiple methods to predict the MNA status based on the CT scans of neuroblastoma patients. A total of 23 patients are enrolled with MNA detection report. To the best of our knowledge, there is no such study in the analysis of CT images in neuroblastoma.

Radiomics-Based Methods. In Table 2, we notice that there is no significant difference in the performance of different ML models. The mean accuracy of the logistic regression model is just 0.04 higher than the AdaBoost model. The results reported in [6] are higher than ours because we report the results on the total validation images rather than the patients. Specifically speaking, we test our model on each tumor slice image and report the accuracy rather than test the model on each patient. If the output of our model is the same as the validation patients number, the mean accuracy of our radiomics-based methods is 0.882 which is 0.06 higher than the 0.826 reported in [6]. In addition, we observe a performance promotion of feature selection as shown in Table 3. When using radiomics-based methods without feature selection, the mean accuracy is 0.72 while with feature selection, the mean accuracy is 0.74. That demonstrates the effectiveness of feature selection which helps the model to focus on the important features.

CNN-Based Methods. Compared to radiomics-based methods, the CNN-based methods achieve higher performance both on the accuracy and AUC. The mean accuracy of CNN-based methods is 0.79 which is 0.05 higher than the best radiomics-based methods.

We notice that, in [7], the results are partly opposite to the results drawn from our experiments. This is likely because of the following reason. [7] uses precisely annotated tumor ROI to extract 3D radiomics features to predict patient outcomes. The 3D features contain more information including the size and shape of the tumor, which helps much to the prediction process. Instead, we do not need the time-consuming segmentation of primal tumors, and CNN focuses on the information of 2D images and performs better on fixed-size images.

As shown in Table 3, we study three approaches to transform gray images into three-channel images. The second approach performs best, and the mean accuracy is 0.06 higher than other approaches. We use the third approach that synthesizes gray images of adjacent slices to three-channel images to capture inter-slices information. However, the performance of this method is worse than the second one. This may be because the original image contains enough information to predict the MNA status.

6   Conclusion

Our study provides insight into that the CNN model has the capability to perform well in the prediction of MNA status of neuroblastoma patient CT scans. In our experiments, the CNN model outperforms multiple radiomics-based ML methods. Different from previous works, we study a much less time-consuming annotation approach which greatly reduces the validation time without manually segmenting primary tumors. We also investigate different approaches to synthesize three-channel images by the original gray images and we find that duplicating the slice image into three-channel images performs better.

Limitation. Due to the computational limitations, we could not perform a study to investigate more CNN models including 3D CNN which may capture inter-slices information better. Also, the radiomics-based methods in our setting is not fully explored. We hope these will inspire future work.

Acknowledgement. This research was supported by HUST Independent Innovation Research Fund (2021XXJS096), Sichuan University Interdisciplinary Innovation Research Fund (RD-03-202108), and the Key Lab of Image Processing and Intelligent Control, Ministry of Education, China.

References

1. Cohn, S.L., et al.: The international neuroblastoma risk group (INRG) classification system: an INRG task force report. J. Clin. Oncol. **27**(2), 289 (2009)
2. Ambros, P.F., et al.: International consensus for neuroblastoma molecular diagnostics: report from the International Neuroblastoma Risk Group (INRG) biology committee. Br. J. Cancer **100**(9), 1471–1482 (2009)
3. Campbell, K., et al.: Association of MYCN copy number with clinical features, tumor biology, and outcomes in neuroblastoma: a report from the children's Oncology Group. Cancer **123**(21), 4224–4235 (2017)
4. Lambin, P., et al.: Radiomics: extracting more information from medical images using advanced feature analysis. Eur. J. Cancer **48**(4), 441–446 (2012)
5. He, K., Zhang, X., Ren, S., Sun, J.: Deep residual learning for image recognition. In: Proceedings of the IEEE Conference on Computer Vision and Pattern Recognition, pp. 770–778 (2016)
6. Wu, H., et al.: Radiogenomics of neuroblastoma in pediatric patients: CT-based radiomics signature in predicting MYCN amplification. Eur. Radiol. **31**(5), 3080–3089 (2020). https://doi.org/10.1007/s00330-020-07246-1
7. Liu, G., et al.: Incorporating radiomics into machine learning models to predict outcomes of neuroblastoma. J. Digital Imaging **2**, 1–8 (2022). https://doi.org/10.1007/s10278-022-00607-w
8. Huang, S.Y., et al.: Exploration of PET and MRI radiomic features for decoding breast cancer phenotypes and prognosis. NPJ Breast Cancer **4**(1), 1–3 (2018)
9. He, K., Zhang, X., Ren, S., Sun, J.: Delving deep into rectifiers: surpassing human-level performance on imagenet classification. In: Proceedings of the IEEE International Conference On Computer Vision, pp. 1026–1034 (2015)
10. Weiss, K., Khoshgoftaar, T.M., Wang, D.D.: A survey of transfer learning. J. Big Data **3**(1), 1–40 (2016). https://doi.org/10.1186/s40537-016-0043-6
11. Wang, S., et al.: Predicting EGFR mutation status in lung adenocarcinoma on computed tomography image using deep learning. Eur. Respir. J. **53**(3) (2019)
12. Di Giannatale, A., et al.: Radiogenomics prediction for MYCN amplification in neuroblastoma: a hypothesis generating study. Pediatr. Blood Cancer **68**(9), e29110 (2021)
13. Yushkevich, P.A., et al.: User-guided 3D active contour segmentation of anatomical structures: significantly improved efficiency and reliability. Neuroimage **31**(3), 1116–28 (2006)
14. Van Griethuysen, J.J., et al.: Computational radiomics system to decode the radiographic phenotype. Can. Res. **77**(21), e104–e107 (2017)

15. Zhang, Z., Xiang, X.: Long-tailed classification with gradual balanced loss and adaptive feature generation. arXiv preprint arXiv:2203.00452 (2022)
16. Hosny, A., Parmar, C., Quackenbush, J., Schwartz, L.H., Aerts, H.J.: Artificial intelligence in radiology. Nat. Rev. Cancer **18**(8), 500–10 (2018)
17. Coroller, T.P., et al.: CT-based radiomic signature predicts distant metastasis in lung adenocarcinoma. Radiother. Oncol. **114**(3), 345–50 (2015)
18. Mackin, D., et al.: Measuring CT scanner variability of radiomics features. Invest. Radiol. **50**(11), 757 (2015)
19. Thawani, R., et al.: Radiomics and radiogenomics in lung cancer: a review for the clinician. Lung Cancer **1**(115), 34–41 (2018)
20. Liu, Z., et al.: Radiomics analysis for evaluation of pathological complete response to neoadjuvant chemoradiotherapy in locally advanced rectal cancer. Clin. Cancer Res. **23**(23), 7253–62 (2017)
21. Liu, Z., et al.: The applications of radiomics in precision diagnosis and treatment of oncology: opportunities and challenges. Theranostics **9**(5), 1303 (2019)

Coordinate Translator for Learning Deformable Medical Image Registration

Yihao Liu[1(✉)], Lianrui Zuo[1,2], Shuo Han[3], Yuan Xue[1], Jerry L. Prince[1], and Aaron Carass[1]

[1] Department of Electrical and Computer Engineering, Johns Hopkins University, Baltimore, MD 21218, USA
yliu236@jhu.edu
[2] Laboratory of Behavioral Neuroscience, National Institute on Aging, National Institute of Health, Baltimore, MD 20892, USA
[3] Department of Biomedical Engineering, Johns Hopkins University, Baltimore, MD 21218, USA

Abstract. The majority of deep learning (DL) based deformable image registration methods use convolutional neural networks (CNNs) to estimate displacement fields from pairs of moving and fixed images. This, however, requires the convolutional kernels in the CNN to not only extract intensity features from the inputs but also understand image coordinate systems. We argue that the latter task is challenging for traditional CNNs, limiting their performance in registration tasks. To tackle this problem, we first introduce Coordinate Translator, a differentiable module that identifies matched features between the fixed and moving image and outputs their coordinate correspondences without the need for training. It unloads the burden of understanding image coordinate systems for CNNs, allowing them to focus on feature extraction. We then propose a novel deformable registration network, `im2grid`, that uses multiple Coordinate Translator's with the hierarchical features extracted from a CNN encoder and outputs a deformation field in a coarse-to-fine fashion. We compared `im2grid` with the state-of-the-art DL and non-DL methods for unsupervised 3D magnetic resonance image registration. Our experiments show that `im2grid` outperforms these methods both qualitatively and quantitatively.

Keywords: Deformable image registration · Deep learning · Magnetic resonance imaging · Template matching

1 Introduction

Deformable registration is of fundamental importance in medical image analysis. Given a pair of images, one fixed and one moving, deformable registration warps the moving image by optimizing the parameters of a nonlinear transformation so that the underlying anatomies of the two images are aligned according to an image dissimilarity function [11,16,32,34,37]. Recent deep learning (DL)

X. Li et al. (Eds.): MMMI 2022, LNCS 13594, pp. 98–109, 2022.
https://doi.org/10.1007/978-3-031-18814-5_10

methods use convolutional neural networks (CNNs) whose parameters are optimized during training; at test time, a dense displacement field that represents the deformable transformation is generated in a single forward pass.

Although CNN-based methods for segmentation and classification are better than traditional methods in both speed and accuracy, DL-based deformable registration methods are faster but usually not more accurate [4,8,13,15,39]. Using a CNN for registration requires learning coordinate correspondences between image pairs, which has been thought to be fundamentally different from other CNN applications because it involves both extracting and matching features [14,25]. However, the majority of existing works simply rely on CNNs to implicitly learn the displacement between the fixed and moving images [4,13,15].

Registration involves both feature extraction and feature matching, but to produce a displacement field, matched features need to be translated to coordinate correspondences. We argue that using convolutional kernels for the latter two tasks is not optimal. To tackle this problem, we introduce Coordinate Translator, a differentiable module that matches features between the fixed and moving images and identifies feature matches as precise coordinate correspondences without the need for training. The proposed registration network, named im2grid, uses multiple Coordinate Translator's with multi-scale feature maps. These produce multi-scale sampling grids representing coordinate correspondences, which are then composed in a coarse-to-fine manner to warp the moving image. im2grid explicitly handles the task of matching features and establishing coordinate correspondence using Coordinate Translator's, leaving only feature extraction to our CNN encoder.

Throughout this paper, we use unsupervised 3D magnetic resonance (MR) image registration as our example task and demonstrate that the proposed method outperforms the state-of-the-art methods in terms of registration accuracy. We think it is important to note that because producing a coordinate location is such a common task in both medical image analysis and computer vision, the proposed method can be impactful on a board range of applications.

2   Related Works

Traditional registration methods solve an optimization problem for every pair of fixed, I_f, and moving, I_m, images. Let ϕ denote a transformation and let the best transformation $\hat{\phi}$ be found from

$$\hat{\phi} = \arg\min_{\phi} L_{\text{sim}}(I_f, I_m \circ \phi) + \lambda L_{\text{smooth}}(\phi), \tag{1}$$

where $I_m \circ \phi$ yields the warped image I_w. The first term focuses on the similarity between I_f and $I_m \circ \phi$ whereas the second term—weighted by the hyperparameter λ—regularizes ϕ. The choice of L_{sim} is application-specific. Popular methods using this framework include spline-based free-form deformable models [32], elastic warping methods [11,27], biomechanical models [16], and Demons [34,37]. Alternatively, learning-based methods have also been used to estimate the transformation parameters [9,19].

Recently, deep learning (DL) methods, especially CNNs, have been used for solving deformable registration problems. In these methods, ϕ is typically represented as a map of displacement vectors that specify the voxel-level spatial offsets between I_f and I_m; the CNN is trained to output ϕ with or without supervision [4,6,13,15,20]. In the unsupervised setting, the displacement field is converted to a sampling grid and the warped image is produced by using a grid sampler [26] with the moving image and the sampling grid as input. The grid sampler performs differentiable sampling of an image (or a multi-channel feature map) using a sampling grid; it allows the dissimilarity loss computed between the warped and fixed images to be back-propagated so the CNN can be trained end-to-end. In past work, [4] used a U-shaped network to output the dense displacement; [12,13] used an encoder network to produce a sparse map of control points and generated the dense displacement field by interpolation; and [8] replaced the bottleneck of a U-Net [31] with a transformer structure [36]. Several deep learning methods also demonstrate the possibility of using a velocity-based transformation representation to enforce a diffeomorphism [10,39].

Our method represents the transformation using a sampling grid G, which can be directly used by the grid sampler. For N-dimensional images ($N = 3$ in this paper), G is represented by an N-channel map. Specifically, for a voxel coordinate $x \in \mathbb{D}^N$ (where $\mathbb{D}^N$ contains all the voxel coordinates in I_f), $G(x)$ should ideally hold a coordinate such that the two values $I_f(x)$ and $I_m(G(x))$ represent the same anatomy. Note that the displacement field representation commonly used by other methods can be found as $G - G_I$, where G_I is the identity grid $G_I(x) = x$.

3   Method

For the image pair I_f and I_m, the proposed method produces a sampling grid G_0 that can be used by the grid sampler to warp I_m to match I_f. Similar to previous DL methods, we use a CNN encoder to extract multi-level feature maps from I_f and I_m. Instead of directly producing a single displacement field from the CNN, G_0 is the composition of multi-level sampling grids, generated from the multi-level feature maps with the proposed Coordinate Translator's.

3.1   Coordinate Translator

Let F and M denote the multi-channel feature maps that are individually extracted from I_f and I_m, respectively. The goal of a Coordinate Translator is to take as input both F and M, and produce a sampling grid G that aligns M interpolated at coordinate $G(x)$ with $F(x)$ for all $x \in \mathbb{D}^N$.

As the first step, for every x, cross-correlation is calculated between $F(x)$ and $M(c_i)$ along the feature dimension, where $c_i \in \mathbb{D}^N$ for $i \in [1, K]$ are a set of candidate coordinates. The results are a K-element vector of matching scores between $F(x)$ and every $M(c_i)$:

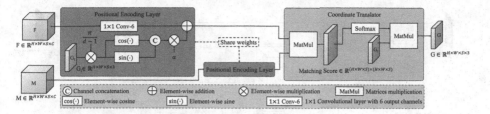

Fig. 1. Structure of the proposed positional encoding layer and Coordinate Translator.

$$\text{Matching Score}(\boldsymbol{x}) = \left(F(\boldsymbol{x})^T M(\boldsymbol{c}_1), \ldots, F(\boldsymbol{x})^T M(\boldsymbol{c}_K)\right). \tag{2}$$

The choice of $\boldsymbol{c}_i$'s determines the search region for the match. For example, defining $\boldsymbol{c}_i$ to be every coordinates in $\mathbb{D}^N$ will compare $F(\boldsymbol{x})$ against every location in M; these matches can also be restricted within the $3 \times 3 \times 3$ neighborhood of $\boldsymbol{x}$. We outline our choices of $\boldsymbol{c}_i$'s in Sect. 4. The matching scores are normalized using a softmax function to produce a matching probability p_i,

$$p_i = \frac{\exp\left(F(\boldsymbol{x})^T M(\boldsymbol{c}_i)\right)}{\sum_j \exp\left(F(\boldsymbol{x})^T M(\boldsymbol{c}_j)\right)} \quad \text{for every } \boldsymbol{c}_i. \tag{3}$$

We interpret the matching probabilities as the strength of attraction between $F(\boldsymbol{x})$ and the $M(\boldsymbol{c}_i)$'s. Importantly, we can calculate a weighted sum of $\boldsymbol{c}_i$'s to produce a coordinate $\boldsymbol{x}' \in \mathbb{R}^N$, i.e., $\boldsymbol{x}' = \sum_{i=1}^{K} p_i \cdot \boldsymbol{c}_i$, which represents the correspondence of $\boldsymbol{x}$ in the moving image I_m. This is conceptually similar to the combined force in the Demons algorithm [34]. For every $\boldsymbol{x} \in \mathbb{D}^N$ the corresponding $\boldsymbol{x}'$ forms the Coordinate Translator output, G.

Coordinate Translator can be efficiently implemented as the Scaled Dot-Product Attention introduced in the Transformer [36] using matrix operations. For 3D images with spatial dimension $H \times W \times S$ and C feature channels, we reshape F and M to $\mathbb{R}^{(H \times W \times S) \times C}$ and the identity grid G_I to $\mathbb{R}^{(H \times W \times S) \times 3}$. Thus Coordinate Translator with $\{\boldsymbol{c}_1, \ldots \boldsymbol{c}_K\} = \mathbb{D}^N$ can be readily computed from,

$$\text{Coordinate Translator}(F, M) = \text{Softmax}(FM^T)G_I, \tag{4}$$

with the softmax operating on the rows of FM^T.

Positional Encoding Layer. In learning transformations, it is a common practice to initialize from (or close to) an identity transformation [4,8,26]. As shown in Fig. 1, we propose a positional encoding layer that combines position information with F and M such that the initial output of Coordinate Translator is an identity grid. Inside a positional encoding layer, for every $\boldsymbol{x} = (x_1, \cdots, x_N)$ with x_i's on an integer grid ($x_i \in \{0, \ldots, d_i-1\}$), we add a positional embedding (PE),

$$\text{PE}(\boldsymbol{x}) = \left(\cos\frac{x_1\pi}{d_1-1}, \sin\frac{x_1\pi}{d_1-1}, \cdots, \cos\frac{x_N\pi}{d_N-1}, \sin\frac{x_N\pi}{d_N-1}\right),$$

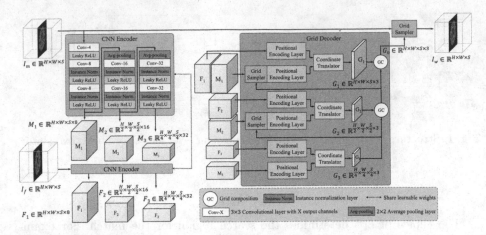

Fig. 2. Example of the proposed `im2grid` network structure with a 3-level CNN encoder. The grid composition operation can be implemented using the grid sampler with two grids as input.

to the input feature map, where d_i is the pixel dimension along the ith axis. Trigonometric identities give the cross-correlation of PEs at x_1 and x_2 as

$$\mathrm{PE}(x_1)^T \mathrm{PE}(x_2) = \sum_{i=1}^{N} \cos\left(\frac{\Delta x_i \pi}{d_i - 1}\right),$$

where Δx_i is the difference in the ith components of x_1 and x_2. This has maximum value when $x_1 = x_2$ and decreases with the L_1 distance between the two coordinates. We initialize the convolutional layer to have zero weights and bias and the learnable parameter $\alpha = 1$ (see Fig. 1) such that only the PEs are considered by Coordinate Translator at the beginning of training. As a result, among all $c_i \in \mathbb{D}^N$, $M(x)$ will have the highest matching score with $F(x)$, thus producing G_I as the initial output. Coordinate Translator also benefits from incorporating the position information as it allows the relative distance between c_i and x to contribute to the matching scores, similar as the positional embedding in the Transformer [36].

3.2   `im2grid` Network Architecture

The proposed `im2grid` network is shown in Fig. 2. Similar to previous methods, `im2grid` produces a sampling grid to warp I_m to I_w. Our CNN encoder uses multiple pooling layers to extract hierarchical features from the intensity images. In the context of intra-modal registration, it is used as a Siamese network that processes I_f and I_m separately. For clarity, Fig. 2 only shows a three level `im2grid` model with three level feature maps $F_1/F_2/F_3$ and $M_1/M_2/M_3$ for I_f and I_m, respectively. In our experiment, we used a five level structure. Our grid decoder uses the common coarse-to-fine strategy in registration. Firstly,

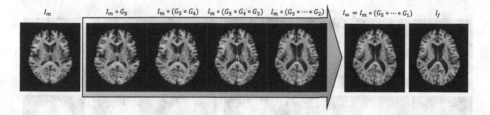

Fig. 3. Visualization of the multi-scale sampling grids by sequentially applying finer grids to the moving image. Here we used a five-level CNN encoder and $G_5, \ldots, G_1$ are coarse to fine sampling grids produced from the five-level feature maps.

coarse features F_3 and M_3 are matched and translated to a coarse sampling grid G_3 using a Coordinate Translator. Because of the pooling layers, this can be interpreted as matching downsampled versions of I_f and I_m, producing a coarse displacement field. G_3 is then used to warp M_2, resolving the coarse deformation between M_2 and F_2 so that the Coordinate Translator at the second level can capture more detailed displacements with a smaller search region. Similarly, M_1 is warped by the composed transformation of G_3 and G_2 and finally the moving image is warped by the composition of the transformations from all levels. A visualization of a five-level version of our multi-scale sampling grids is provided in Fig. 3. In contrast to previous methods that use CNNs to directly output displacements, our CNN encoder only needs to extract similar features for corresponding anatomies in I_f and I_m and the exact coordinate correspondences are obtained by Coordinate Translator's. Because our CNN encoder processes I_f and I_m separately, it is guaranteed that our CNN encoder only performs feature extraction.

The proposed network is trained using the mean squared difference between I_f and $I_w (= I_m \circ \phi)$ and a smoothness loss that regularizes the spatial variations of the G's at every level,

$$\mathcal{L} = \frac{1}{|\mathbb{D}^N|} \sum_{\boldsymbol{x} \in \mathbb{D}^N} (I_f(\boldsymbol{x}) - I_w(\boldsymbol{x}))^2 + \lambda \sum_i \sum_{\boldsymbol{x} \in \mathbb{D}^N} ||\nabla (G_i(\boldsymbol{x}) - G_I(\boldsymbol{x}))||^2, \quad (5)$$

where $|\mathbb{D}^N|$ is the cardinality of $\mathbb{D}^N$ and all G_i's and G_I are normalized to $[-1, 1]$.

4   Experiments

Datasets. We used the publicly available OASIS3 [28] and IXI [1] datasets in our experiments. 200, 40, and 100 T1-weighted (T1w) MR images of the human brain from the OASIS3 dataset were used for training, validation, and testing, respectively. During training, two scans were randomly selected as I_f and I_m, while validation and testing used 20 and 50 pre-assigned image pairs, respectively. For the IXI dataset, we used 200 scans for training, 20 and 40 pairs for

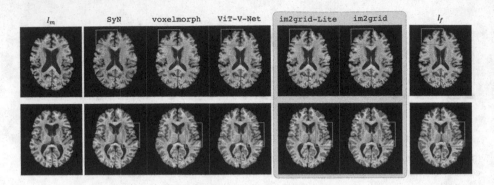

Fig. 4. Examples of registering the moving image (the first column) to the fixed image (the last column) using SyN, voxelmorph, ViT-V-Net, and our proposed methods.

validation and testing, respectively. All scans underwent N4 inhomogeneity correction [35], and were rigidly registered to MNI space [18] with 1 mm^3 (for IXI) or 0.8 mm^3 (for OASIS3) isotropic resolution. A white matter peak normalization [30] was applied to standardize the MR intensity scale.

Evaluation Metrics. First, we calculated the Dice similarity coefficient (DSC) between segmentation labels of I_f and the warped labels of I_m. An accurate transformation should align the structures of the fixed and moving images and produces a high DSC. We obtained a whole brain segmentation for the fixed and moving images using SLANT [24] and combined the SLANT labels (133 labels) to TOADS labels (9 labels) [5]. The warped labels were produced by applying each methods deformation field to the moving image labels. Second, we measured the regularity of the transformations by computing the determinant of the Jacobian matrix, which should be globally positive for a diffeomorphic transformation.

Implementation Details. Our method was implemented using PyTorch and trained using the Adam optimizer with a learning rate of 3×10^{-4}, a weight decay of 1×10^{-9}, and a batch size of 1. Random flipping of the input volumes along the three axes were used as data augmentation. We used a five-level structure and tested different choices of c_i's for each Coordinate Translator. We found that given the hierarchical structure, a small search region at each level is sufficient to capture displacements presented in our data. Therefore, we implemented two versions of our method: 1) im2grid which used a 3×3 search window in the axial plane for producing G_1 and a $3 \times 3 \times 3$ search window at other levels; and 2) im2grid-Lite which is identical to im2grid except that the finest grid G_1 is not used.

Baseline Methods: We compared our method with several state-of-the-art DL and non-DL registration methods: 1) SyN: Symmetric image normalization method [2], implemented in the Advanced Normalization Tools (ANTs) [3];

Table 1. The Dice coefficient (DSC), the average number of voxels with negative determinant of Jacobian (# of $|J_\phi| < 0$) and the percentage of voxels with negative determinant of Jacobian (%) for affine transformation, SyN, Voxelmorph, ViT-V-Net, and the proposed methods. The results of the initial alignment by the preprocessing steps are also included. Bold numbers indicate the best DSC for each dataset.

	OASIS3			IXI		
	DSC	# of $|J_\phi| < 0$	%	DSC	# of $|J_\phi| < 0$	%
Initial	0.651 ± 0.094	–	0%	0.668 ± 0.107	–	0%
Affine	0.725 ± 0.068	–	0%	0.748 ± 0.052	–	0%
SyN [2]	0.866 ± 0.029	223	<0.002%	0.845 ± 0.035	613	0.008%
Voxelmorph [4]	0.883 ± 0.040	85892	<0.7%	0.842 ± 0.068	21574	<0.3%
ViT-V-Net [8]	0.872 ± 0.042	110128	<0.9%	0.845 ± 0.068	21298	<0.2%
im2grid-Lite	$\mathbf{0.909 \pm 0.021}$	38915	<0.4%	$\mathbf{0.870 \pm 0.043}$	14917	<0.2%
im2grid	0.908 ± 0.023	11880	<0.1%	0.865 ± 0.050	3235	<0.04%

2) voxelmorph: A deep learning based unsupervised method trained with the mean squared error loss [4]; 3) ViT-V-Net: A transformer [36] based network structure proposed in [8].

For SyN, a wide range of hyper-parameters were tested on the OASIS3 validation set and the best performing parameters were used for generating the final results. For voxelmorph and ViT-V-Net, we adopted the same training strategies as the proposed method, including the loss function and data augmentation. We optimize the parameters of each method for performance on the OASIS3 validation set and then used those parameters in testing on both datasets.

Results. For both OASIS3 and IXI test datasets, we registered the moving to the fixed image and report the averaged DSC for all labels in Table 1. In both datasets, the proposed methods outperform the comparison methods for DSC. For each individual anatomic label, we also conducted a paired, two-sided Wilcoxon signed rank test (null hypothesis: the difference between paired values comes from a distribution with zero median, $\alpha = 10^{-3}$) between our methods and the comparison methods. Both proposed methods show significant DSC improvements for seven of nine labels and comparable DSC performance to the best comparison method for the remaining two labels (thalamus and putamen). Visual examples on OASIS3 data are shown in Fig. 4. It can be seen, especially from the highlighted regions, that the warped image produced by the proposed methods have a better agreement with the fixed image.

Evaluation on Learn2Reg Validation Dataset. We also test the proposed method on the inter-subject brain MRI registration task from the Learn2Reg challenge [22] (L2R 2021 Task 3). All scans from the challenge have been pre-processed following [23], and for evaluation purpose segmentation maps of 35 labels were generated using FreeSurfer [17]. We choose the im2grid-Lite version for this task because the challenge evaluation is done on the ×2 downsampled

Table 2. Results of the proposed method and several state-of-the-art methods on the Learn2Reg 2021 Task 3 validation dataset.

	DSC	DSC30	SDlogJ	HD95
im2grid-Lite	0.8729 ± 0.0142	0.8714	0.1983	1.3786
TransMorph [7]	0.8691 ± 0.0145	0.8663	0.0945	1.3969
ConvexAdam [33]	0.8464 ± 0.0159	0.8460	0.0668	1.5003
Han *et al.* [21]	0.8410 ± 0.0139	0.8355	0.0796	1.6595
Lv *et al.* [29]	0.8271 ± 0.0131	0.8199	0.1206	1.7220

images. During training, two scans were randomly selected from the training set and used as input to the proposed method. The performance is evaluated by comparing the warped segmentation of the moving image and the segmentation of the fixed image. The results are summarized in Table 2, where the DSC represents the average Dice coefficient of all segmented labels; DSC30 is the lowest 30% DSC among all cases, which measures the robustness of the methods; SDlogJ is the standard deviation of the log of the Jacobian determinant of the deformation field; and HD95 represents the 95% percentile of Hausdorff distance of segmentations. The results of several state-of-the-art methods from the challenge leaderboard are also included. The proposed method shows better accuracy as well as robustness among the comparison methods. Although adopting the instance-specific optimization as described in [4] can potential boost the performance on the validation set, our method only used the training set because we assume that such fine tuning process is not available during deployment.

5   Discussion

In this paper, we proposed Coordinate Translator for producing coordinate correspondences from two feature maps. Additionally, we proposed the im2grid network that uses Coordinate Translator's for deformable image registration. For unsupervised 3D magnetic resonance registration, im2grid outperforms the state-of-the-art methods in accuracy with a similar training and testing speed as other deep learning based registration methods. Although im2grid has no explicit guarantee of being diffeomorphic, the deformation fields it generated contains fewer voxels with negative determinant of Jacobian compared with other deep learning methods that output deformation fields directly from feature maps. We believe this comes from our design decision to restrict the candidate voxels to the immediate neighborhood of a voxel, which yields a locally smooth deformation field at each scale. We note that even a diffeomorphic algorithm with theoretical guarantees (*e.g.,* SyN) can produce non-diffeomorphic transformations because of errors introduced during interpolation [38].

For registration, we demonstrated that using Coordinate Translator for matching features and establishing coordinate correspondences together with the convolutional networks for feature extraction can significantly boost the performance. Coordinate Translator is a general module that can be incorporated in many existing network structures and therefore is not limited to the registration task. We believe that many tasks that involve image input and coordinate output can benefit from the use of the Coordinate Translator module.

Acknowledgement. This work was supported in part by the NIH/NEI grant R01-EY032284 and the Intramural Research Program of the NIH, National Institute on Aging.

References

1. IXI Brain Development Dataset. https://brain-development.org/ixi-dataset/
2. Avants, B.B., Epstein, C.L., Grossman, M., Gee, J.C.: Symmetric diffeomorphic image registration with cross-correlation: evaluating automated labeling of elderly and neurodegenerative brain. Med. Image Anal. **12**(1), 26–41 (2008)
3. Avants, B.B., Tustison, N., Song, G., et al.: Advanced normalization tools (ANTS). Insight J. **2**(365), 1–35 (2009)
4. Balakrishnan, G., Zhao, A., Sabuncu, M.R., Guttag, J., Dalca, A.V.: VoxelMorph: a learning framework for deformable medical image registration. IEEE Trans. Med. Imaging **38**(8), 1788–1800 (2019)
5. Bazin, P.L., Pham, D.L.: Topology-preserving tissue classification of magnetic resonance brain images. IEEE Trans. Med. Imaging **26**(4), 487–496 (2007)
6. Cao, X., et al.: Deformable image registration based on similarity-steered CNN regression. In: Descoteaux, M., Maier-Hein, L., Franz, A., Jannin, P., Collins, D.L., Duchesne, S. (eds.) MICCAI 2017. LNCS, vol. 10433, pp. 300–308. Springer, Cham (2017). https://doi.org/10.1007/978-3-319-66182-7_35
7. Chen, J., Frey, E.C., He, Y., Segars, W.P., Li, Y., Du, Y.: TransMorph: transformer for unsupervised medical image registration. arXiv preprint arXiv:2111.10480 (2021)
8. Chen, J., He, Y., Frey, E.C., Li, Y., Du, Y.: ViT-V-Net: vision transformer for unsupervised volumetric medical image registration. arXiv preprint arXiv:2104.06468 (2021)
9. Chou, C.R., Frederick, B., Mageras, G., Chang, S., Pizer, S.: 2D/3D image registration using regression learning. Comput. Vis. Image Underst. **117**(9), 1095–1106 (2013)
10. Dalca, A.V., Balakrishnan, G., Guttag, J., Sabuncu, M.R.: Unsupervised learning for fast probabilistic diffeomorphic registration. In: Frangi, A.F., Schnabel, J.A., Davatzikos, C., Alberola-López, C., Fichtinger, G. (eds.) MICCAI 2018. LNCS, vol. 11070, pp. 729–738. Springer, Cham (2018). https://doi.org/10.1007/978-3-030-00928-1_82
11. Davatzikos, C.: Spatial transformation and registration of brain images using elastically deformable models. Comput. Vis. Image Underst. **66**(2), 207–222 (1997)
12. De Vos, B.D., Berendsen, F.F., Viergever, M.A., Sokooti, H., Staring, M., Išgum, I.: A deep learning framework for unsupervised affine and deformable image registration. Med. Image Anal. **52**, 128–143 (2019)
13. de Vos, B.D., Berendsen, F.F., Viergever, M.A., Staring, M., Išgum, I.: End-to-end unsupervised deformable image registration with a convolutional neural network. In: Cardoso, M.J., et al. (eds.) DLMIA/ML-CDS -2017. LNCS, vol. 10553, pp. 204–212. Springer, Cham (2017). https://doi.org/10.1007/978-3-319-67558-9_24

14. Dosovitskiy, A., et al.: FlowNet: learning optical flow with convolutional networks. In: Proceedings of the IEEE International Conference on Computer Vision, pp. 2758–2766 (2015)
15. Fan, J., Cao, X., Yap, P.T., Shen, D.: BIRNet: brain image registration using dual-supervised fully convolutional networks. Med. Image Anal. **54**, 193–206 (2019)
16. Ferrant, M., Warfield, S.K., Nabavi, A., Jolesz, F.A., Kikinis, R.: Registration of 3D intraoperative MR images of the brain using a finite element biomechanical model. In: Delp, S.L., DiGoia, A.M., Jaramaz, B. (eds.) MICCAI 2000. LNCS, vol. 1935, pp. 19–28. Springer, Heidelberg (2000). https://doi.org/10.1007/978-3-540-40899-4_3
17. Fischl, B.: FreeSurfer. NeuroImage **62**(2), 774–781 (2012)
18. Fonov, V., Evans, A., McKinstry, R., Almli, C., Collins, D.: Unbiased nonlinear average age-appropriate brain templates from birth to adulthood. Neuroimage **47**, S102 (2009)
19. Gutiérrez-Becker, B., Mateus, D., Peter, L., Navab, N.: Learning optimization updates for multimodal registration. In: Ourselin, S., Joskowicz, L., Sabuncu, M.R., Unal, G., Wells, W. (eds.) MICCAI 2016. LNCS, vol. 9902, pp. 19–27. Springer, Cham (2016). https://doi.org/10.1007/978-3-319-46726-9_3
20. Han, R., et al.: Deformable MR-CT image registration using an unsupervised end-to-end synthesis and registration network for endoscopic neurosurgery. In: Medical Imaging 2021, vol. 11598, p. 1159819. International Society for Optics and Photonics (2021)
21. Han, R., et al.: Deformable MR-CT image registration using an unsupervised end-to-end synthesis and registration network for endoscopic neurosurgery. In: Medical Imaging 2021: Image-Guided Procedures, Robotic Interventions, and Modeling, vol. 11598, p. 1159819. International Society for Optics and Photonics (2021)
22. Hering, A., et al.: Learn2Reg: comprehensive multi-task medical image registration challenge, dataset and evaluation in the era of deep learning. arXiv preprint arXiv:2112.04489 (2021)
23. Hoopes, A., Hoffmann, M., Fischl, B., Guttag, J., Dalca, A.V.: HyperMorph: amortized hyperparameter learning for image registration. In: Feragen, A., Sommer, S., Schnabel, J., Nielsen, M. (eds.) IPMI 2021. LNCS, vol. 12729, pp. 3–17. Springer, Cham (2021). https://doi.org/10.1007/978-3-030-78191-0_1
24. Huo, Y., et al.: 3D whole brain segmentation using spatially localized atlas network tiles. Neuroimage **194**, 105–119 (2019)
25. Ilg, E., et al.: FlowNet 2.0: evolution of optical flow estimation with deep networks. In: Proceedings of the IEEE Conference on Computer Vision and Pattern Recognition, pp. 2462–2470 (2017)
26. Jaderberg, M., Simonyan, K., Zisserman, A., et al.: Spatial transformer networks. In: Advances in Neural Information Processing Systems, vol. 28 (2015)
27. Klein, S., Staring, M., Murphy, K., Viergever, M.A., Pluim, J.P.: Elastix: a toolbox for intensity-based medical image registration. IEEE Trans. Med. Imaging **29**(1), 196–205 (2009)
28. LaMontagne, P.J., et al.: OASIS-3: longitudinal neuroimaging, clinical, and cognitive dataset for normal aging and Alzheimer disease. MedRxiv (2019)
29. Lv, J., et al.: Joint progressive and coarse-to-fine registration of brain MRI via deformation field integration and non-rigid feature fusion. IEEE Trans. Med. Imaging (2022)
30. Reinhold, J.C., et al.: Evaluating the impact of intensity normalization on MR image synthesis. In: Medical Imaging 2019: Image Processing, vol. 10949, p. 109493H. International Society for Optics and Photonics (2019)

31. Ronneberger, O., Fischer, P., Brox, T.: U-Net: convolutional networks for biomedical image segmentation. In: Navab, N., Hornegger, J., Wells, W.M., Frangi, A.F. (eds.) MICCAI 2015. LNCS, vol. 9351, pp. 234–241. Springer, Cham (2015). https://doi.org/10.1007/978-3-319-24574-4_28

32. Rueckert, D., Sonoda, L.I., Hayes, C., Hill, D.L., Leach, M.O., Hawkes, D.J.: Non-rigid registration using free-form deformations: application to breast MR images. IEEE Trans. Med. Imaging **18**(8), 712–721 (1999)

33. Siebert, H., Hansen, L., Heinrich, M.P.: Fast 3D registration with accurate optimisation and little learning for Learn2Reg 2021. In: Aubreville, M., Zimmerer, D., Heinrich, M. (eds.) MICCAI 2021. LNCS, vol. 13166, pp. 174–179. Springer, Cham (2022). https://doi.org/10.1007/978-3-030-97281-3_25

34. Thirion, J.P.: Image matching as a diffusion process: an analogy with Maxwell's demons. Med. Image Anal. **2**(3), 243–260 (1998)

35. Tustison, N.J., et al.: N4ITK: improved N3 bias correction. IEEE Trans. Med. Imaging **29**(6), 1310–1320 (2010)

36. Vaswani, A., et al.: Attention is all you need. In: Advances in Neural Information Processing Systems, vol. 30 (2017)

37. Vercauteren, T., Pennec, X., Perchant, A., Ayache, N.: Diffeomorphic demons: efficient non-parametric image registration. Neuroimage **45**(1), S61–S72 (2009)

38. Wyburd, M.K., Dinsdale, N.K., Namburete, A.I.L., Jenkinson, M.: TEDS-Net: enforcing diffeomorphisms in spatial transformers to guarantee topology preservation in segmentations. In: de Bruijne, M., et al. (eds.) MICCAI 2021. LNCS, vol. 12901, pp. 250–260. Springer, Cham (2021). https://doi.org/10.1007/978-3-030-87193-2_24

39. Yang, X., Kwitt, R., Styner, M., Niethammer, M.: Quicksilver: fast predictive image registration–a deep learning approach. Neuroimage **158**, 378–396 (2017)

Towards Optimal Patch Size in Vision Transformers for Tumor Segmentation

Ramtin Mojtahedi[1] , Mohammad Hamghalam[1,2] , Richard K. G. Do[3] ,
and Amber L. Simpson[1,4(✉)]

[1] School of Computing, Queen's University, Kingston, ON, Canada
`amber.simpson@queensu.ca`
[2] Department of Electrical Engineering, Qazvin Branch,
Islamic Azad University, Qazvin, Iran
[3] Department of Radiology, Memorial Sloan Kettering Cancer Center,
New York, NY, USA
[4] Department of Biomedical and Molecular Sciences,
Queen's University, Kingston, ON, Canada

Abstract. Detection of tumors in metastatic colorectal cancer (mCRC) plays an essential role in the early diagnosis and treatment of liver cancer. Deep learning models backboned by fully convolutional neural networks (FCNNs) have become the dominant model for segmenting 3D computerized tomography (CT) scans. However, since their convolution layers suffer from limited kernel size, they are not able to capture long-range dependencies and global context. To tackle this restriction, vision transformers have been introduced to solve FCNN's locality of receptive fields. Although transformers can capture long-range features, their segmentation performance decreases with various tumor sizes due to the model sensitivity to the input patch size. While finding an optimal patch size improves the performance of vision transformer-based models on segmentation tasks, it is a time-consuming and challenging procedure. This paper proposes a technique to select the vision transformer's optimal input multi-resolution image patch size based on the average volume size of metastasis lesions. We further validated our suggested framework using a transfer-learning technique, demonstrating that the highest Dice similarity coefficient (DSC) performance was obtained by pre-training on training data with a larger tumour volume using the suggested ideal patch size and then training with a smaller one. We experimentally evaluate this idea through pre-training our model on a multi-resolution public dataset. Our model showed consistent and improved results when applied to our private multi-resolution mCRC dataset with a smaller average tumor volume. This study lays the groundwork for optimizing semantic segmentation of small objects using vision transformers. The implementation source code is available at: https://github.com/Ramtin-Mojtahedi/OVTPS.

Keywords: CT segmentation · Vision transformer · Liver tumor

X. Li et al. (Eds.): MMMI 2022, LNCS 13594, pp. 110–120, 2022.
https://doi.org/10.1007/978-3-031-18814-5_11

1   Introduction

Colorectal cancer is the third most common cancer diagnosed in the United States, with 100,000 new cases and 50,000 deaths expected in 2022 [1]. The survival rate of these patients is over 90% [2]. However, up to 70% of them will develop liver metastasis [3], with a roughly 5-year survival rate of 11% [4]. The segmentation of metastatic colorectal cancer (mCRC) liver tumours on computed tomography (CT) images is essential for evaluating tumour response to chemotherapy and surgical planning [5], especially for detecting small metastasis tumor volumes in the liver tissue. To achieve this objective, it is imperative to build and develop a reliable and automated machine-learning (ML) model.

Convolutional neural networks (CNNs)-based [6–10] and vision transformers (ViTs)-based [11] architectures are the major machine learning segmentation approaches. Since the introduction of the pioneering U-shaped encoder-decoder architecture, dubbed U-Net [12], CNN-based architectures have achieved state-of-the-art performance on a variety of medical image segmentation tasks [13]. The U-Net is a densely supervised encoder-decoder network where the encoder and decoder sub-networks are connected by densely supervised skip pathways. Adapting the U-Net to new challenges entails a range of design, preprocessing, training, and assessment strategies for the network. These hyperparameters are interconnected and have a substantial effect on the outcome. The nnU-Net framework was developed by Isensee et al. [14] to address these limitations. Based on 2D and 3D vanilla U-Nets, they suggested nnU-Net as a robust and self-adaptive architecture.

Despite the effectiveness of fully convolutional networks, these networks have a drawback in learning global context and long-range spatial relationships due to their confined kernel size and receptive fields. To tackle this limitation, Dosovitsky et al. [15] proposed using transformers in computer vision tasks, called ViTs, resulting from their successful performance in the language domain, their ability to capture long-range dependencies, and their self-attention mechanisms. Compared to state-of-the-art convolutional networks, ViT-based models achieve significant outcomes while using fewer computing resources for the training phase. By integrating an additional control mechanism in the self-attention module, a gated axial-attention model was presented by Valanarasu et al., [16], extending the previous transformer-based architectures. A novel ViT-based on a hierarchical structure was introduced by Liu et al. [17] to represent the image features through shifted windows. Their proposed structure improved performance as self-attention processing is limited to non-overlapping local windows, but cross-window connections are still allowed. Hatamizadeh et al. [18] proposed UNEt TRansformers (UNETR) to capture global multi-scale information. This unique U-Net-based architecture employs a transformer as the encoder to learn sequence representations of the input volume. The extracted features from the transformer encoder are integrated with the CNN-based decoder through skip connections to predict the segmentation outputs.

Although the UNETR achieved state-of-the-art performance in 3D volumetric segmentation, it used an isotropic network topology with fixed-size feature resolution and an inflexible embedding size. Therefore, UNETR could not describe context at various sizes or assign computations at different resolutions. While their proposed network could be performant for segmenting large-sized objects such as the liver, it did not show the same level of performance in segmenting small objects such as small liver tumors.

Our goal in this paper was to detect and segment colorectal liver metastases on abdominal CT scans. The contribution of this work is twofold: First, we introduce a framework to find an optimal patch size for the vision transformer models to improve ViT-based structures in segmenting small objects. Specifically, based on the liver lesion volume, we designed a framework for ViT patch size, using the UNETR architecture as the backbone of our experiments to achieve higher segmentation performance. We also validated our proposed framework in a transfer-learning approach and showed that pre-training on training data that has a larger tumor volume using the proposed optimal patch size and then training with a smaller one achieved the best Dice similarity coefficient (DSC) performance. Second, we show that our pipeline outperforms the UNETR baseline ViT-based model in terms of DSC for segmenting liver metastasis and validates our results on LiTS and mCRC datasets.

2   Method

In the following subsections, the structure of the ViT-based model, our procedure to select optimal patch size, and a novel training technique to improve performance on segmenting of small tumors are elaborated.

2.1   ViT-Based Model Structure

Transformer Patch. In the ViT transformer framework, the input image is split into patches, and a series of linear embeddings of these patches is passed to the vanilla transformer [15]. These image patches are processed and considered similar to tokens (words) in natural language processing. Specifically, transformers operate on a 1D sequence of input embeddings. Similarly, the given 3D input images are mapped to 1D embedding vectors in our pipeline. In the utilized framework, the 3D CT volumes are provided with an input size of (H, W, L) are the input image dimensions. The transformer patches are represented as M. Accordingly, flattened uniform sequences are being created with the size of $N = (H \times W \times L)/(M \times M \times M)$ using non-overlapping patches that are shown with $y_v \in R^{N \times M^3}$.

To maintain the retrieved patches' spatial information, 1D learnable positional embeddings ($\mathbf{E}_{pos} \in R^{N \times P}$) are added to the projected patch embeddings with dimensional embedding size. This process is shown in Eq. (1).

$$\mathbf{z}_0 = [y_v^1\mathbf{E}; y_v^2\mathbf{E}; ...; y_v^N\mathbf{E}] + \mathbf{E}_{pos} \tag{1}$$

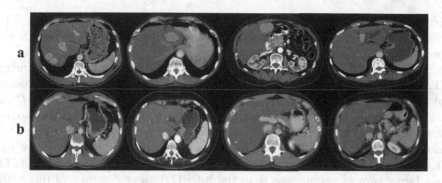

Fig. 1. Comparing tumor sizes in mCRC and LiTS sample data where (a) is the LiTS dataset with larger tumor volume size, and (b) is the mCRC dataset (Green: liver, Yellow: tumor). (Color figure online)

where $\mathbf{E} \in R^{M^3 \times P}$ is flattened uniform non-overlapping patches embedding [13]. The transformer encoder consists of alternating layers of multi-headed self-attention (MSA) and multilayer perceptron (MLP) blocks. As proposed in [9], these blocks can be shown as Eq. (2) and Eq. (3).

$$\acute{z}_j = \mathbf{MSA}(\mathbf{Lnorm}(\mathbf{z}_{j-1})) + \mathbf{z}_{j-1}, j \in [1, ..., T] \tag{2}$$

$$\acute{z}_j = \mathbf{MLP}(\mathbf{Lnorm}(\acute{z}_j)) + \acute{z}_j, j \in [1, ..., T] \tag{3}$$

where T is the number of transformer layers, *Lnorm* function denotes layer normalization, and the MLP block consists of two linear layers with GELU activation functions. There are parallel self-attention (SA) heads in the MSA sublayer, and attention weights are calculated as (4). The SA block uses standard **qkv** self-attention, which uses query (**q**) and the sequence's associated key (**k**) and input sequence value (**v**) representations. Equation (4) is also included where $K_h = K/n$ is the scaling factor and the outputs of the MSA are achieved as Eq. (5) using MSA weights ($\mathbf{W}_{MSA} \in R^{n \cdot K_h \times S}$).

$$\text{Attention}(\mathbf{q}, \mathbf{k}, \mathbf{v}) = \text{Softmax}(\frac{\mathbf{q}\mathbf{K}^T}{\sqrt{K_h}})\mathbf{v} \tag{4}$$

$$[\mathbf{Attention}_1(z); ...; \mathbf{Attention}_n(z)]\mathbf{W}_{MSA} \tag{5}$$

Loss Function. The loss function employed is a mix of soft Dice loss and cross-entropy loss, which could be calculated in a voxel-by-voxel approach, as shown in Eq. (6).

$$Loss(G, O) = 1 - \frac{2}{C}\sum_{r=1}^{C}\frac{\Sigma_{x=1}^{A}G_{x,r}O_{x,r}}{\Sigma_{x=1}^{C}G_{x,r}^2 + \Sigma_{K=1}^{U}O_{x,r}^2} - \frac{1}{A}\sum_{x=1}^{A}\sum_{r=1}^{C}G_{x,r}log(O_{x,r}) \tag{6}$$

where A represents the voxel's number; C denotes the number of classes. The probability output and one-hot encoded ground truth for class r at voxel x are represented by $O_{x,r}$ and $G_{x,r}$, respectively [19].

UNETR uses a contracting-expanding pattern with a stack of transformers, ViT, as the encoder, and skip connections to the decoder. It considers the patch size as a hyperparameter. In this sense, choosing an optimal patch size (M^*) is critical due to its impact on the features' receptive field. This is because patches are reshaped into a tensor with the size of $\frac{H}{M^*} \times \frac{W}{M^*} \times \frac{L}{M^*} \times P$, where P is the transformer's embedding size. To assess the impact of patch size, we did our experiments on two clinical datasets, LiTS, and our private mCRC. LiTS has a larger tumors volume size than the mCRC dataset. Samples of these two datasets are shown in Fig. 1.

2.2   Choosing Optimal Patch Size

The proposed framework tries to find the best patch size for our tumor segmentation. As shown in Fig. 2, the average volume of the tumors is first computed on the training input. Then, the optimal patch size is determined based on a mathematical relationship between the average volume size of tumors and the performance. The experimented patch sizes must be a factor of the input image dimensions, $256 \times 256 \times 96$, and were selected based on our computational resources and with respect to the sizes proposed in [15], $M \in [8, 12, 16, 24]$. This ensures that the model performs best when segmenting small objects such as tumors.

The average volume size of tumors in LiTS datasets was reported as 17.56 cm^3 [20]. Through histogram analysis on our private mCRC dataset, the average tumor volume was achieved as 10.42 cm^3. Empirically, the relationship between optimal patch size (M^*) and the average volume size of the tumors attained as Eq. (7).

$$M^* = \underset{M \in [8,12,16,24]}{\text{Argmin}} \ (|\sqrt[3]{V \times S} - M|) \tag{7}$$

where M is the patch size; S is the voxel spacing, and V is the average volume size of tumors for LiTS and mCRC datasets. The optimal patch is achieved by finding the patch that makes the absolute differentiation of cube root multiplication of voxel spacing and average tumors volume size with patch size be at a minimum.

2.3   Pre-training Technique to Improve Segmentation of Small Tumors

To increase the segmentation performance of ViT-based structures on small lesions, we suggested pre-training on a dataset with a large tumor volume (LiTS data) using the optimal patch size achieved by the proposed framework and subsequently training on a smaller one (mCRC dataset) to achieve the best DSC performance. This idea was experimentally tested, as shown in the next section, and could increase the DSC significantly compared to when the dataset with a small tumor volume was trained by scratch.

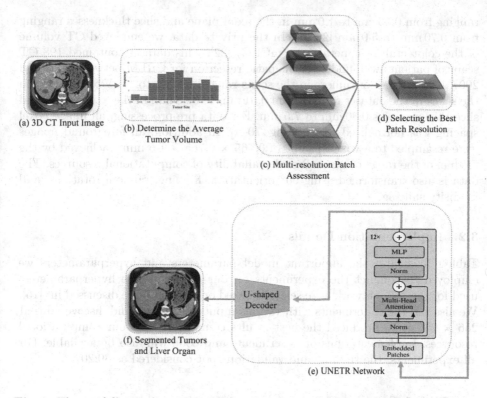

(a) 3D CT Input Image

(b) Determine the Average Tumor Volume

(c) Multi-resolution Patch Assessment

(d) Selecting the Best Patch Resolution

(f) Segmented Tumors and Liver Organ

(e) UNETR Network

Fig. 2. The model's pipeline is shown for the proposed framework. In step (a), the framework receives the raw 3D CT images of the abdomen, consisting of the liver and its primary and secondary tumors. Then, the average tumor volume is computed through histogram analysis in step (b). Through assessment of the averaged volume of tumors and the three determined patch sizes in step (c), $M \in [8, 12, 16, 24]$ the optimal patch size is selected in step (d). In step (e), we train the model and segment it in our backboned UNETR network to achieve segmented tumors and liver organs in step (f).

3   Experimental Results

3.1   Datasets

We conducted our experiments on two multi-resolution 3D abdominal CT liver datasets, including training with large tumor volumes (LiTS) and later smaller ones (mCRC). For the former, we used the LiTS, which consisted of 201 CT images with liver and liver tumors annotations: 131 for training and 70 for testing. The number of tumors detected in the scans varied between 0 and 75, exhibiting a half-normal distribution. The dataset was created to closely show real-world clinical data and contains a range of cancer types, including primary tumors such as hepatocellular carcinoma (HCC) and metastasis from colorectal, breast, and lung cancer. The collection includes scans with voxel spacings ranging from 0.56 mm to 1.0 mm in the axial plane and slice thicknesses ranging from 0.70 mm to 5.0 mm [20,21]. In the private data, we employed CT volume of the colorectal liver metastasis (mCRC) [22]. This dataset contained 198 CT scans of patients who underwent hepatic resection for CRLM between 2003 and 2007. The number of tumors in the scans ranged from 1 to 17. Voxel spacing in the scans in the dataset ranged from 0.61 mm to 0.98 mm in the axial plane, and slice thickness was 0.80 mm to 7.5 mm. For data pre-processing, all image voxel spacing was normalized to the range [0–1]. In addition, all foreground images were resampled to a voxel spacing of $0.765 \times 0.765 \times 1.5$ mm^3, achieved by the median of the range of spacings and availability of computational resources. The data is also transformed using 90° orientation, flipping, random rotations, and intensity shifting.

3.2   Implementation Details

Table 1 illustrates the important model parameters and hyperparameters we employed to conduct the experiments on our datasets. The hyperparameters used for the ViT network were selected based on the ViT-base discussed in [15]. We also ran the experiments with various input image sizes and discovered that $256 \times 256 \times 96$ produced the best results compatible with our computational resources. Implementations of experiments and code will also be available. For all experiments, the training and validation split considered as 80:20.

Table 1. Summary of employed parameters and critical hyperparameters.

Parameter	Description of the value/method
Input image size [H × W × L]	[256 × 256 × 96]
Optimizer	Adam
Learning rate	0.0001
Weight-decay	1e−5
ViT: [Layers, Hidden Size, MLP size, Heads, Number of Parameters]	[12, 768, 3072, 12, 86M]
Batch Size	1
Computational resource	NVIDIA A100 - 40 GB

3.3   Liver and Lesion Segmentation Results

Segmentation Results for Optimal Patch size. We calculated the optimal patch size, M^*, based on Eq. (7) for both datasets. We also compared our results with smaller and larger patch sizes than the calculated one to validate our proposed technique. As shown in Table 2, the best performance results were achieved for the computed patch size of 16 and 12 for the LiTS and mCRC datasets, respectively. In addition to these experiments, we tested the DSC performance using a combination of both datasets, which did not outperform the following results. Moreover, as our main focus was to find the optimal patch size, we didn't provide results with respect to the CNN-based architectures, which inherently have different structures with no utilized transformer.

Table 2. Highest segmentation performance results for the models built on LiTS and mCRC datasets using multiple patch sizes.

Dataset	Patch size	Tumor DSC [%]	Liver DSC [%]	Loss	Training time [Min.]
LiTS	M = 8	48.62	81.3	0.2105	1883.93
	M = 12	51.19	87.37	0.2297	2464.83
	M* = 16	**53.08**	**88.06**	**0.1805**	**2811.70**
	M = 24	51.91	87.93	0.1717	4106.87
mCRC	M = 8	39.64	89.51	0.1893	3745.30
	M* = 12	**41.44**	**92.35**	**0.1020**	**2221.24**
	M = 16	40.14	87.77	0.1060	2566.82
	M = 24	38.82	87.85	0.2050	3758.87

Effectiveness of the Proposed Vision-Based Model Training. Table 3 indicates that employing LiTS pre-trained models significantly improves segmentation performance. The patch size of 16 showed the best outcomes, with a DSC of 44.94% for tumor segmentation. This indicates that training on a large tumor volume dataset successfully learns tumor representations that improve model performance on an mCRC dataset with small tumor volume mCRC.

Table 3. Comparison of the highest segmentation performance (DSC (%)) results using the pre-trained model on the dataset with larger tumor volumes (LiTS) to the dataset with smaller tumor volumes (mCRC).

Patch size	Pre-trained model		Non pre-trained model		Improvement	
	Tumor	Liver	Tumor	Liver	Tumor	Liver
8	42.2	93.97	39.64	89.51	2.56	4.46
12	44.46	94.42	41.44	92.35	3.02	2.07
16 (M*)	**44.94**	**94.61**	**40.14**	**87.77**	**4.8**	**6.84**

Figure 3 visually compares the segmentation performance between pre-trained models on the LiTS dataset with larger tumor volumes to the mCRC dataset with smaller tumor volumes both for tumor and liver organ.

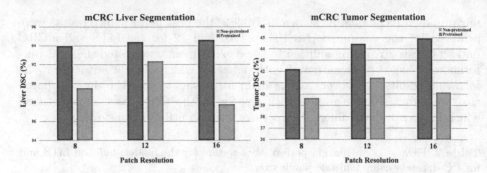

Fig. 3. The performance results for the tumor and liver organ segmentation tasks were obtained using LiTS pre-trained models and mCRC itself for training. All pre-trained models could improve performance, while the model with a patch size of 16 achieved the best results, improving the tumor segmentation performance by 4.8%.

4 Discussion and Conclusion

This paper proposed a novel framework to find an optimal patch size for semantic segmentation, particularly practical for small liver lesion segmentation. Based on the volume size of metastasis, we introduced a procedure to calculate patch size methodically in transformer-based segmentation models. In addition, the optimal patch size computed by the proposed method showed the best performance on large objects such as a liver organ. Furthermore, a significant part of the small tumor information was missed when we trained on a large patch size. However, when we pre-trained a model on our public dataset of LiTS with larger tumors, the model could learn tumors representations with higher performance. Consistent with our first novelty and in a transfer-learning approach, the pre-trained model demonstrated its most effective performance in learning representations and segmentation performance when it utilized the computed optimal patch size defined by (7), M^*. The results of this study could be used for further development in vision transformer-based networks with multi-patch sizes. We also showed that our pipeline outperforms the ViT-based models in terms of DSC for segmenting liver metastasis tumors and validated our results on LiTS and mCRC datasets.

Acknowledgement. This work was funded in part by National Institutes of Health R01CA233888.

References

1. Colorectal cancer - statistics. https://www.cancer.net/cancer-types/colorectal-cancer/statistics. Accessed 31 May 2022
2. Colorectal cancer survival rates: Colorectal cancer prognosis. https://www.cancer.org/cancer/colon-rectal-cancer/detection-diagnosis-staging/survival-rates. Accessed 1 Mar 2022

3. Liver metastases (secondary liver cancer). https://www.mskcc.org/cancer-care/types/liver-metastases
4. Valderrama-Treviño, A.I., Barrera-Mera, B., Ceballos-Villalva, J.C., Montalvo-Javé, E.E.: Hepatic metastasis from colorectal cancer. Eur. J. Hepato-Gastroenterol. **7**, 166–175 (2016).https://doi.org/10.5005/jp-journals-10018-1241
5. Wu, W., Wu, S., Zhou, Z., Zhang, R., Zhang, Y.: 3D liver tumor segmentation in CT images using improved fuzzy c-means and graph cuts. BioMed. Res. Int. 1–11 (2017). https://doi.org/10.1155/2017/5207685
6. Soleymanifard, M., Hamghalam, M.: Segmentation of whole tumor using localized active contour and trained neural network in boundaries. In: 2019 5th Conference on Knowledge Based Engineering and Innovation (KBEI) (2019)
7. Hamghalam, M., Wang, T., Qin, J., Lei, B.: Transforming intensity distribution of brain lesions via conditional GANs for segmentation. In: 2020 IEEE 17th International Symposium on Biomedical Imaging (ISBI) (2020)
8. Hamghalam, M., Lei, B., Wang, T.: Convolutional 3D to 2D patch conversion for pixel-wise glioma segmentation in MRI scans. In: Crimi, A., Bakas, S. (eds.) BrainLes 2019. LNCS, vol. 11992, pp. 3–12. Springer, Cham (2020). https://doi.org/10.1007/978-3-030-46640-4_1
9. Hamghalam, M., Frangi, A.F., Lei, B., Simpson, A.L.: Modality completion via gaussian process prior variational autoencoders for multi-modal glioma segmentation. In: de Bruijne, M., et al. (eds.) MICCAI 2021. LNCS, vol. 12907, pp. 442–452. Springer, Cham (2021). https://doi.org/10.1007/978-3-030-87234-2_42
10. Hamghalam, M., Lei, B., Wang, T.: High tissue contrast MRI synthesis using multi-stage attention-GAN for segmentation. In: Proceedings of the AAAI Conference on Artificial Intelligence, vol. 34, pp. 4067–4074 (2020)
11. Zheng, S., et al.: Rethinking semantic segmentation from a sequence-to-sequence perspective with Transformers. In: 2021 IEEE/CVF Conference on Computer Vision and Pattern Recognition (CVPR) (2021)
12. Ronneberger, O., Fischer, P., Brox, T.: U-net: convolutional networks for biomedical image segmentation. In: Navab, N., Hornegger, J., Wells, W.M., Frangi, A.F. (eds.) MICCAI 2015. LNCS, vol. 9351, pp. 234–241. Springer, Cham (2015). https://doi.org/10.1007/978-3-319-24574-4_28
13. Zhou, Z., Rahman Siddiquee, M.M., Tajbakhsh, N., Liang, J.: UNet++: a nested U-net architecture for medical image segmentation. In: DLMIA/ML-CDS -2018. LNCS, vol. 11045, pp. 3–11. Springer, Cham (2018). https://doi.org/10.1007/978-3-030-00889-5_1
14. Isensee, F., Jaeger, P.F., Kohl, S.A., Petersen, J., Maier-Hein, K.H.: NNU-net: a self-configuring method for deep learning-based biomedical image segmentation. Nat. Methods **18**, 203–211 (2020). https://doi.org/10.1038/s41592202001008z
15. Dosovitskiy, A., et al.: An image is worth 16 × 16 words: transformers for image recognition at scale. In: ICLR 2021 (2021)
16. Valanarasu, J.M.J., Oza, P., Hacihaliloglu, I., Patel, V.M.: Medical transformer: gated axial-attention for medical image segmentation. In: de Bruijne, M., et al. (eds.) MICCAI 2021. LNCS, vol. 12901, pp. 36–46. Springer, Cham (2021). https://doi.org/10.1007/978-3-030-87193-2_4
17. Liu, Z., et al.: Swin transformer: hierarchical vision transformer using shifted windows. arXiv preprint arXiv: 2103.14030 (2021)
18. Hatamizadeh, A., et al.: UNETR: transformers for 3D medical image segmentation. In: 2022 IEEE/CVF Winter Conference on Applications of Computer Vision (WACV) (2022)

19. Milletari, F., Navab, N., Ahmadi, S.-A.: V-net: fully convolutional neural networks for volumetric medical image segmentation. In: 2016 Fourth International Conference on 3D Vision (3DV) (2016). https://doi.org/10.1109/3DV.2016.79
20. Antonelli, M., et al.: The medical segmentation decathlon. Nat. Commun. **13**, 1–13 (2022)
21. Bilic, P., et al.: The liver tumor segmentation benchmark (LiTS). arXiv preprint arXiv:1901.04056 (2019)
22. Simpson, A.L., et al.: Computed tomography image texture: a noninvasive prognostic marker of hepatic recurrence after hepatectomy for metastatic colorectal cancer. Ann. Surg. Oncol. **24**, 2482–2490 (2017)

Improved Multi-modal Patch Based Lymphoma Segmentation with Negative Sample Augmentation and Label Guidance on PET/CT Scans

Liangchen Liu[1(✉)], Jianfei Liu[1], Manas Kumar Nag[1], Navid Hasani[1], Seung Yeon Shin[1], Sriram S. Paravastu[1], Babak Saboury[1], Jing Xiao[2], Lingyun Huang[2], and Ronald M. Summers[1]

[1] Imaging Biomarkers and Computer-Aided Diagnosis Laboratory, Radiology and Imaging Sciences, Clinical Center, National Institutes of Health, Bethesda, MD, USA
liangchen.liu@nih.gov
[2] Ping An Technology, Shenzhen, China

Abstract. Lymphoma is a cancer of the lymphatic system, and it can affect many organs throughout the body. Positron emission tomography (PET)/computed tomography (CT) are primary imaging methods to assess lymphoma types and monitor their treatment, where PET is sensitive to identify lymphoma regions while CT preserves anatomical structures. Combining PET and CT is thus useful for lymphoma segmentation because it helps to identify lymphoma types and evaluate treatment effects. However, lymphoma segmentation suffers many challenges, including substantial lymphoma size and shape variance, numerous types, limited PET/CT data for lymphoma, and similar PET signals with adjacent organs. To address these challenges, we integrate label guidance, patch sampling, and negative data augmentation to achieve multi-modal lymphoma segmentation. The training data consist of positive and negative patch samples. These samples are purposely extracted from the original scans with the guidance of lymphoma labels. Negative samples are further supplemented from the PET/CT scans of non-lymphoma patients to better discriminate lymphoma from adjacent organs. The proposed method was validated on the PET/CT scans from 28 patients. Experimental results revealed that the Dice coefficient was improved from 0.11 to 0.43 in comparison with a baseline method the 3D-residual U-Net method. Patch-based strategy is also computational undemanding. These results suggest that the proposed method could be an efficient means to segment lymphoma and possibly used for identifying lymphoma types and assessing their treatment.

Keywords: Multi-modal · PET-CT · Lymphoma · Patch-based

© The Author(s), under exclusive license to Springer Nature Switzerland AG 2022
X. Li et al. (Eds.): MMMI 2022, LNCS 13594, pp. 121–129, 2022.
https://doi.org/10.1007/978-3-031-18814-5_12

1   Introduction

Lymphoma is a hematopoietic malignancy with numerous types, and it can affect people of all ages [1]. Lymphoma treatment response is highly dependent on the measurement of tumor burden, which often requires accurate identification of lymphoma regions. Positron emission tomography (PET)/computed tomography (CT) [2,4,8] are primary imaging methods to assess lymphoma and monitor treatment response. Figure 1 illustrates an example of PET/CT scans on lymphoma patient. Organs such as kidney and liver are well depicted, but lymphoma is difficult to identify in the CT scan (Left Image). In contrast, the standardized uptake value (SUV) is used to measure fluorodeoxyglucose positron emission tomography uptake or glucose metabolism of the tumor regions in the PET scan. For this reason, lymphoma is visually represented as bright regions in the PET scan (yellow arrows) while organs are hard to delineate. These observations motivate us to develop a multi-modal lymphoma segmentation method as it is useful for lymphoma treatment.

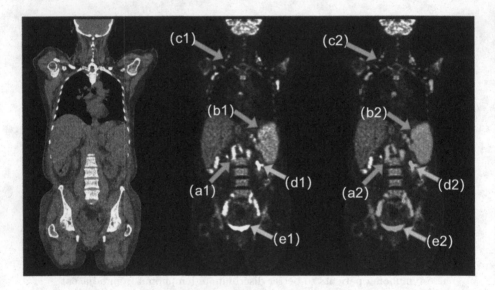

Fig. 1. Example of lymphoma distributed on the paired PET-CT scans. **Left column**: organs are preserved in the CT scan; **Center column**: lymphoma is highlighted with bright regions in the PET scan (yellow arrows), in which it is randomly spread to the whole body; **Right column**: PET scan with overlayed lymphoma labels, from which we can observe that lymphomas are outside organs (a1, a2), inside organs (b1, b2), small spots (c1, c2). Kidneys (d1, d2) and bladder (e1, e2) could also have bright normal regions similar to lymphoma. All these challenges are attributed to the difficulty of lymphoma segmentation.

However, lymphoma segmentation is a challenging task because it can randomly spread throughout the body (Fig. 1). It could be either outside organs (a1, a2) or inside organs (b1, b2). Lymphoma also has a wide range of shapes and sizes, such as tiny spots (c1, c2). High SUV values at kidneys (d1, d2) and bladder (e1, e2) are also similar to those at lymphoma. All these difficulties hinder lymphoma segmentation, and only a limited number of methods have been developed for lymphoma segmentation. An ensemble model from DeepMedic was developed for pediatric lymphoma PET/CT scans [11]. DenseX-Net was also developed to segment lymphoma on the whole-body PET/CT scans [7]. However, the input of these methods is 2D slice, which potentially lose the spatial coherence among slices. Another 3D segmentation method based on the belief function was used to segment lymphoma [3], which integrated a feature extraction module and an evidential segmentation (ES) module. Although it achieved decent segmentation results, it has not considered the multi-scale and patch-based framework to further extract the useful information from the details of the PET and CT scans. This paper aims to develop a deep learning-based approach to segment lymphoma on multimodal PET/CT scans. Our method combines Label guided Patch sampling for Multi-Modalities, and negative sample augmentation (LPMM-nsa) to serve the segmentation purpose. The training data are composed of a set of local image patches, and positive (green boxes, Fig. 2), and negative patches (red boxes, Fig. 2) are extracted according to the likelihood of lymphoma regions or non-lymphoma regions. In other words, positive samples are more likely from the lymphoma regions and negative samples are from non-lymphoma regions, which could help to create high-quality data for training. Negative samples are further enhanced from PET/CT scans of non-lymphoma patients[1] to better discriminate the lymphoma from organs. Since our method is patch based, the proposed method is naturally computationally undemanding and GPU memory efficient, which is suitable for clinical applications. A validation dataset with 28 lymphoma patients is also created to evaluate the segmentation accuracy, in which the lymphoma size changes drastically, and they are more close to the real clinical practice.

2   Method

For demonstration of the effectiveness of the proposed methods, we choose to use the widely validated 3D-residual U-Net as the back-bone structure to develop our own modules (Fig. 2). It is noted that the proposed methods can be extended to other more advanced structure in simple plug-in fashion such as [3].

2.1   Notation and Formation

Let us first give some notations and formations to improve readability. Multi-modal PET/CT dataset $\{\mathbf{X}_i\}_{i=1}^n$ where $\mathbf{X}_i$ is a sample in the dataset, which channel-wise concatenates the PET and CT modalities. Training and testing datasets are defined as $\{\mathbf{X}_i^t\}_{i=1}^k$ and $\{\mathbf{X}_i^v\}_{i=1}^l$ respectively. Their corresponding

---

[1] https://clinicaltrials.gov/ct2/show/NCT01724749.

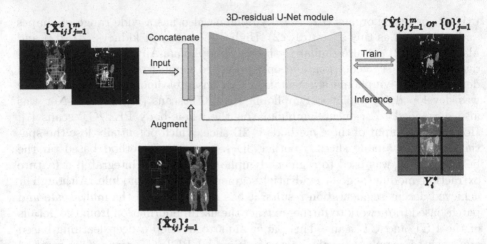

Fig. 2. Overview of the proposed lymphoma segmentation method based on 3D-residual U-Net. Positive patch samples (green boxes) are extracted from the lymphoma regions guided by their labels, and negative samples (red boxes) are created from non-lymphoma regions. (Color figure online)

labels are, thus, given as $\{\mathbf{Y}_i^t\}_{i=1}^k$ and $\{\mathbf{Y}_i^v\}_{i=1}^l$. Each element y in $\mathbf{Y}_i^t$ and $\mathbf{Y}_i^v$ belongs to the set $\{0,1\}$ denoting lymphoma and non-lymphoma regions, respectively. Let us denote the 3D residual U-Net as $\mathbf{E}$ and the loss function as $\mathcal{L}$. Then the classic segmentation framework is as follows:

$$\theta^* = \min_{\theta(\mathbf{E})} \sum_{i=1}^k \mathcal{L}(\mathbf{E}(\mathbf{X}_i^t), \mathbf{Y}_i^t) \tag{1}$$

where $\theta(\mathbf{E})$ stands for the trainable parameters of the network and θ^* is the optimized parameters of the network.

2.2   Label-Guided Patch Sampling

To further extract the useful information from the details of the PET/CT scans and decrease the computing resource demanding issue of the huge 3D volumetric data, we utilize the strategies of label-guided patch sampling. Training samples are extracted based on the guidance of data label. The sampling function S() extracts patches non-homogeneously in terms of probability of the presence of lymphoma guided by the label map $\mathbf{Y}_i^t$ because lymphoma regions and their adjacent regions should be highlighted. The sampling process is thus given by:

$$\{\hat{\mathbf{X}}_{ij}^t\}_{j=1}^m = \mathrm{S}(\mathbf{X}_i^t; \mathbf{f}, m, \mathbf{Y}_i^t) \tag{2}$$

where the $\hat{\mathbf{X}}_{ij}^t$ represents the j-th patch sampled from the scan dataset $\mathbf{X}_i^t$. m indicates the number of patches. The $\mathbf{f}$ Bernoulli distribution to sample the images from the lymphoma and non-lymphoma regions according to the $\mathbf{Y}_i^t$:

$$\mathbf{f}(y;p) = \begin{cases} p & \text{if } y = 1, \\ 1-p & \text{if } y = 0. \end{cases} \tag{3}$$

where the probability p is set as 0.6 in this work, and $y = 1$ if it is a positive sample and $y = 0$ if it is a negative sample. Using patch sampling leads (1) to:

$$\theta^* = \min_{\theta(\mathbf{E})} \sum_{i=1,j=1}^{n,m} \mathcal{L}(\mathbf{E}(\hat{\mathbf{X}}_{ij}^t), \hat{\mathbf{Y}}_{ij}^t) \tag{4}$$

where $\hat{\mathbf{Y}}_{ij}^t$ is the patch label of $\hat{\mathbf{X}}_{ij}^t$.

2.3 Negative Sample Augmentation

Negative sample augmentation is another efficient strategy to enhance the training data. PET/CT scans of the non-lymphoma patients were used for discriminating organs from lymphoma. Therefore, we denote the extra patch dataset as $(\{\hat{\mathbf{X}}_{ij}^e\}_{j=1}^s, \{\mathbf{0}\}_{j=1}^s)$, where the negative patches $\{\hat{\mathbf{X}}_{ij}^e\}_{j=1}^s$ are randomly sampled from the extra negative samples $\{\mathbf{X}_i^e\}_{i=1}^q$. The symbol $\mathbf{0}$ means the all 0 label tensor for the negative sample $\hat{\mathbf{X}}_{ij}^e$. Finally, our framework is expressed as:

$$\theta^* = \min_{\theta(\mathbf{E})} \sum_{i=1,j=1}^{n,m} \mathcal{L}(\mathbf{E}(\hat{\mathbf{X}}_{ij}^t), \hat{\mathbf{Y}}_{ij}^t) + \sum_{i=1,j=1}^{q,s} \mathcal{L}(\mathbf{E}(\hat{\mathbf{X}}_{ij}^e), \mathbf{0}) \tag{5}$$

Optimizing (5) yields the trained network $\mathbf{E}^*$. During inference, the prediction of the patches of a PET/CT scans is given by $\hat{\mathbf{Y}}_{ij}^* = \mathbf{E}^*(\hat{\mathbf{X}}_{ij}^v)$. These predicted patches are stitched based on the aggregation function:

$$\mathbf{Y}_i^* = G(\hat{\mathbf{X}}_{ij}^*; \alpha) \tag{6}$$

where the α represents the parameters for the patch aggregation, which includes patch size, overlap margin, and $\mathbf{Y}_i^*$ is the final lymphoma segmentation.

The ADAM optimizer [6] with weight decay is used for training. The learning rate is set to 10^{-3}. The proposed method is implemented in PyTorch. Both training and testing are performed on the Nvidia DGX station equipped with a Tesla A100 graphics card with 40 GB GPU memory.

2.4 Data Collection and Validation Methods

Twenty-two lymphoma patients underwent whole body (WB) PET and CT examinations between 2010–2021 were collected, and Research Consortium for Medical Image Analysis (RECOMIA) AI tool was used to initially label the lymphoma regions. These labeled results were then reviewed and manually corrected by an experienced radiology residence. Labeled results were eventually confirmed by a nuclear medicine physician, which generates our lymphoma labels.

All twenty-two PET/CT scans were resampled to $500 \times 500 \times 850$ pixels through cropping and padding operations. The intensity is normalized to $[0, 1]$ using the window range of $[-1000, 800]$ on the CT scan and the SUV window range of $[0, 40]$ inspired by [10] on PET scan. We empirically set the patch size as $64 \times 64 \times 64$. For the SUV computation, we use the SUV normalized by the body weight (SUVbw) [5][2]. More specifically, the computation method is listed as follows:

$$SUVbw = (PET\ image\ Pixels) * (weight\ in\ grams)/(injected\ dose) \quad (7)$$

PET image pixels and injected dose are decay corrected to the start of scan. After the conversion, the pet image pixels are in units (g/ml). Three metrics are used for validation, including Dice score (dsc), average symmetric surface distance (assd), and sensitivity. Two experiments were conducted in this work. The first is the comparison between the baseline 3D residual U-Net and the proposed method with different settings, including the proposed label guided patch sampling for multi-modal data (LPMM), and its further improved version with negative sample augmentation (LPMM-nsa). The second is the comparison among single modality (PET or CT only) and multi-modal (PET/CT).

3   Experiments

The comparison of segmentation results using different methods is reported in Table 1. It reveals that the combination of label guidance, patch sampling and negative data augmentation (LPMM-nsa) achieves the highest segmentation accuracy. It also suggested that the input of multi-modal data is another key component to improve the segmentation accuracy as the dice-coefficient is only 0.11 using PET scan only. In contrast, the proposed method can achieve 0.43.

Comparison results in Fig. 3 also supported these findings because the baseline 3D residual U-Net is prone to over-segmenting lymphoma (second row). In contrast, over-segmentation is substantially reduced after using label guidance and patch sampling. However, it could induce the issue of under-segmentation, which was further improved by the addition of negative sample augmentation. Figure 4 also proves the importance of multi-modal input. All lymphomas are missed from the model trained on CT scans only because lymphoma is non-trivial to identify on CT scans. Some lymphoma were segmented using the model with PET scans only, and the segmentation results were vastly improved with both modalities. Since CT and PET concentrate on the different parts of lymphoma patients, they might contribute to each other to more accurately identify lymphoma regions.

To further demonstrate the advantage of our methods, we illustrate several results from each multi-modal method in details in Fig. 3 from axial.

---

[2] https://qibawiki.rsna.org/index.php/Standardized_Uptake_Value_(SUV).

Table 1. Comparison of lymphoma segmentation results using different methods

	dsc↑	assd↓	sensitivity↑
Single modality			
3D-residual U-Net (Pet only)	0.11	29.8	0.3
Multiple modalities			
3D-residual U-Net	0.18	41.4	0.82
LPMM (ours)	0.26	28.95	**0.84**
LPMM-nsa (ours)	**0.43**	**19.12**	0.82

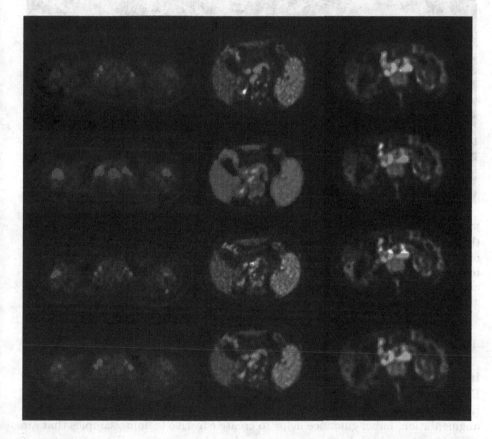

Fig. 3. Comparison of lymphoma segmentation results using different segmentation models. The three columns show slices from three scans respectively. First row: ground truth; second row: segmentation results from the baseline 3D-residual U-Net method where lymphomas are over-segmented; third row: results from the segmentation model enhanced with label guided patch sampling where over-segmentation is substantially reduced but with some lymphoma under-segmentated; fourth row: results with the addition of negative sample augmentation, in which lymphomas are accurately segmented.

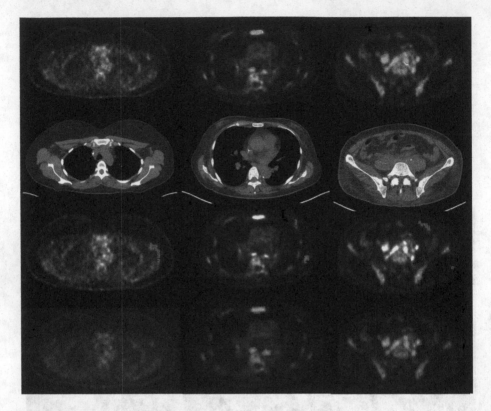

Fig. 4. Comparison of lymphoma segmentation using different image modalities. The three columns show slices from three scans respectively. First row: ground truth, second row: segmentation results using CT only, third row: results using PET only, and fourth row: results using both CT and PET. No lymphomas are segmented on CT scans only, and some lymphomas are found in the results with PET only. Almost all lymphomas are segmented using both modalities

4   Conclusion and Future Work

In this paper, we developed a multi-modal lymphoma segmentation method on PET/CT scans. Three key components were integrated to improve the segmentation accuracy, including label guidance, patch sampling, and negative sample augmentation. Label guidance helps to create effective training samples that are more focused on both lymphoma and non-lymphoma regions. Patch samples not only reduces computational cost, but also avoid over-segmentation from the baseline 3D residual U-Net (third row, Fig. 3). Negative sample augmentation could further reduce the issue of under-segmentation raised by path sampling (fourth row, Fig. 3). Comparing with the segmentation models from single modal, multi-modal is another important property to the segmentation accuracy (Fig. 4. The validation results in Table 1 also proved that the proposed method utilized all effective means to achieve the highest segmentation accuracy.

In the future, we would like to explore more about the multiple modality fusion methods, such as graph-based methods [9], multimodal transformers [12], as well as incorporate additional modal of clinical reports to continuously improve segmentation accuracy. Nevertheless, the proposed method shows the promising results to accurately segment lymphoma on PET/CT scans.

Acknowledgements. This research was supported by the National Institutes of Health, Clinical Center and by a Cooperative Research and Development Agreement with Ping An.

References

1. A predictive model for aggressive Non-Hodgkin's lymphoma. N. Engl. J. Med. **329**(14), 987–994 (1993). https://doi.org/10.1056/NEJM199309303291402
2. Czernin, J., Allen-Auerbach, M., Nathanson, D., Herrmann, K.: PET/CT in oncology: current status and perspectives. Curr. Radiol. Rep. **1**(3), 177–190 (2013)
3. Huang, L., Ruan, S., Decazes, P., Denœux, T.: Evidential segmentation of 3D PET/CT images. In: Denœux, T., Lefèvre, E., Liu, Z., Pichon, F. (eds.) BELIEF 2021. LNCS (LNAI), vol. 12915, pp. 159–167. Springer, Cham (2021). https://doi.org/10.1007/978-3-030-88601-1_16
4. Juweid, M.E., Cheson, B.D.: Positron-emission tomography and assessment of cancer therapy. N. Engl. J. Med. **354**(5), 496–507 (2006)
5. Kim, C.K., Gupta, N.C., Chandramouli, B., Alavi, A.: Standardized uptake values of FDG: body surface area correction is preferable to body weight correction. J. Nucl. Med. **35**(1), 164–167 (1994)
6. Kingma, D.P., Ba, J.: Adam: a method for stochastic optimization. In: Bengio, Y., LeCun, Y. (eds.) 3rd International Conference on Learning Representations, ICLR 2015, San Diego, CA, USA, 7–9 May 2015, Conference Track Proceedings (2015). http://arxiv.org/abs/1412.6980
7. Li, H., et al.: DenseX-Net: an end-to-end model for lymphoma segmentation in whole-body PET/CT images. IEEE Access **8**, 8004–8018 (2019)
8. Li, J., Xiao, Y.: Application of FDG-PET/CT in radiation oncology. Front. Oncol. **3**, 80 (2013)
9. Liu, L., Nie, F., Wiliem, A., Li, Z., Zhang, T., Lovell, B.C.: Multi-modal joint clustering with application for unsupervised attribute discovery. IEEE Trans. Image Process. **27**(9), 4345–4356 (2018)
10. Noy, A., et al.: The majority of transformed lymphomas have high standardized uptake values (SUVs) on positron emission tomography (PET) scanning similar to diffuse large b-cell lymphoma (DLBCL). Ann. Oncol. **20**(3), 508–512 (2009)
11. Weisman, A.J., et al.: Automated quantification of baseline imaging pet metrics on FDG PET/CT images of pediatric Hodgkin lymphoma patients. EJNMMI Phys. **7**(1), 1–12 (2020)
12. Xu, P., Zhu, X., Clifton, D.A.: Multimodal learning with transformers: a survey. arXiv preprint arXiv:2206.06488 (2022)

Author Index

Printed in the United States
by Baker & Taylor Publisher Services

Printed in the United States
by Baker & Taylor Publisher Services